To Sheena,

Best Wishes

NOT QUITE FAMOUS

Recollections and travels of a female singer

1966 to 1986

CAROLE JARDINE

aka

CAROLE St. JAMES

Published by Honeybee Books
Broadoak, Dorset
www.honeybeebooks.co.uk

Printed in the UK using paper from sustainable sources

ISBN: 978-1-910616-48-2

For my wonderful children, Alex and Annabelle

CONTENTS

PROLOGUE

On the morning of September 7th 1982 my life was turned upside down, when this previously "non famous" singer found herself splashed across the front page of The Sun newspaper under the auspicious headline "*A Handful For Andy*" with more photos filling the centre page spread under the banner headline "*NAUTICAL BUT NICE – Randy Andy's ocean wave rave with the dancing girls*" referring to my act, Carole St. James and 'Dream' who had recently returned from the South Atlantic entertaining HM Forces, including HRH Prince Andrew and the officers and crew of *HMS Invincible* following the Falklands War.

My first reaction was shock and I put the paper to one side and didn't actually read it properly for another twenty-four hours. When I did, I threw up. I'm still not sure whether it was the size and sensationalism of the spread, the inaccuracies of the report, being outrageously misquoted, or that this "singer" was referred to as "sexy dancer Carole" that upset me the most.

It didn't stop there of course, other newspapers picked up on the story and the fact that my boyfriend at the time was Radio 2 disc jockey David Hamilton just added to the madness with around ten more days of photos, headlines and ridiculous stories, that is until the next "Andrew" story came out and Koo Stark became the new target; then it died as quickly as it had begun.

Fame for 10 days – I didn't like it.

Chapter 1

BEGINNINGS

My singing career began very simply in 1966.

I was working at the time in a Manchester advertising agency and was always singing, even in the office. No-one seemed to mind, my bosses Tom and Joan Phillips were quite eccentric and my colleagues were an interesting, creative and humorous bunch. One day a secretary who had recently joined the company came into the office and promptly joined in my song, harmonising beautifully. "Wow" I said, "that sounded good. Perhaps we should form an act and travel around the world singing. Do you play any instruments?"

"Only the piano" came the reply,

"That's no good – we couldn't cart that around with us" I joked. However, we became friends and found we lived quite close to one another. Her name was Anna and she was Polish. Her family were all musical and so I started going to her home at least twice a week in the evening, where her mother would play the piano and teach Anna, her younger sister Maria and myself songs, some of them Polish (which I learned phonetically) and we would sing in three part harmony. It wasn't long before we were asked to sing at the Polish Club in Manchester. Then we were asked to perform at a function in the Embassy Rooms in Sale, so we looked around for a guitar player, as up until then, Anna had played guitar (she'd not been entirely honest about only playing the piano). A lady who worked part time at the same ad. agency said her son could play guitar, so we got together with him for a while, but although very willing, he was only a beginner and not really up to the job, one evening playing the whole of a song called Freight Train in the wrong key. We always looked back on that show as the night we derailed Freight Train! At first we called ourselves The New World Singers, (we were quite folksy), then tried The Carnivals, but as we did more gigs, found ourselves a more experienced and capable guitarist by the name of John Hampson and changed our image, wearing more glamorous costumes, we finally settled on the name The Starlettes.

As the Starlettes we appeared in venues in and around Manchester for a while and one memorable evening we appeared at a private function in the Midland Hotel, Manchester with Tony Bookbinder's orchestra (Tony was a cousin of Elke Brooks), for a very large party of Jewish pensioners. The audience were appreciative, quiet and polite throughout the performance until our last song which was Hava Nagila when, to our amazement, walking sticks went flying as elderly gentlemen leapt to their feet and, aches and pains forgotten, clapped, danced, twirled and sang along to the music. They would not let us leave the stage until we sang it one more time and we finally exited to thunderous applause and hearty cheering from the then exhausted, but supremely happy seniors.

But it wasn't long before love stepped in and lured Anna away to marry her soldier sweetheart Mike and head off for his posting in Cyprus, leaving Maria and I as a duo. Our guitarist John said he knew of another guitar player called Lenny Mervyn who he invited along to one of our rehearsals, Lenny was enthusiastic and we liked him and so we started to put together a four piece act, but soon after Maria also decided show business was not for her and she bowed out. John came to the rescue again however, saying he knew of another musician, an excellent vibraphone player called Bill Conway, who was trying to get a more jazz style duo together with a girl singer - sixth former Liz Oldfield and suggested we all meet up.

We all got together one evening, did a bit of jamming and a lot of talking and decided we could combine to form a 5-piece group doing pops and standards with jazz overtones and plenty of harmony singing. And thus began a period of very happy music making, friendship and growing success as a group.

Chapter 2

LES BLUESETTES

We called ourselves Les Bluesettes (which we thought sophisticated), unfortunately we sometimes found ourselves billed in northern clubs as "Les and the Bluesettes", even being asked on one occasion "Which one is Les?" We usually practiced twice a week (we all had day jobs then except Liz who was studying for her 'A' levels), and we began to produce a harmonious and unique sound.

A dear friend of mine, John Bennett, a comedy impressionist whose professional name was Johnny Martin, was keen to help us and he introduced us to his management - comedy scriptwriters Wilf Fielding and Steve Nelson who also performed as a comedy double act known as "Nelson & Fields". Apart from being really nice guys, Wilf and Steve proved invaluable to us, giving advice on stage presentation, microphone techniques, professional presentation etc. and getting us gigs, frequently accompanying us to performances and helping us to hone the act. Wilf once told us that when he was standing at the back of an auditorium as we were performing the song"Mrs Robinson" at a showcase (a show put on for booking agents to view acts), he overheard one booker remark on our professionalism to another, who replied "yes - they must be American."

One day they arranged for us to do an audition for BBC Radio. The "Beeb" used to record artistes themselves in those days to broadcast "live" music as well as playing records on the Light Programme (as it was then). The producer who listened to us that day was Peter Pilbeam. We set up on the stage of the BBC theatre in Hulme, Manchester and performed "Mrs Robinson". As we finished the number Peter Pilbeam literally ran all the way from the back of the auditorium and asked "How long have you been together to produce a sound like that?"

"Six months" we answered.

"Amazing" he said "have you got any more songs?"

We played some more and he instantly booked us to record them for BBC Radio. We recorded four songs in all, in just one take each as we were so well rehearsed and "tight" and these were later broadcast on programmes like "Roundabout" over the next few months. As far as we were concerned we were just doing what we enjoyed most, looking back, I don't think any of us realised how good the act was.

Les Bluesettes became more and more popular in clubs in the North West and Yorkshire and we played lots of gigs as there were so many venues then, In 1969 we won an award for best group in the Club Acts of the Year Awards put on by the Manchester branch of Equity. Liz had left school by then, having passed her 'A' levels and John, Bill and I all left our jobs as we could not manage all the gigs and work during the day as well, so became fully professional. We all had our Equity cards by then too. Our first fully professional gig was a week in Morecambe, supporting the P.J. Proby Show, which we watched after our own spot. It was a very good show and though I didn't know it at the time, was not to be the last time I would come across the legendary Jim Proby. Our week in Morecambe went well and lots more offers of work followed. We appeared in a variety of venues from northern working men's clubs and other social clubs to smart cabaret clubs of which there were loads in the North and Midlands at that time.

Disaster almost struck when Liz's parents decided to move away to Chelmsford and expected Liz to go with them. Happily my folks came to the rescue and offered Liz a home with us in order to keep the act together and fortunately her parents agreed, so Liz came to stay.

The act had some interesting moments in social clubs. Once our show was interrupted mid song by a ringing telephone that was situated in a box on the stage, we had to stop singing as the club chairman answered the phone and then began giving out the pigeon racing results while we all stood quietly behind him, trying hard not to laugh. He then turned to us and said "carry on", which we dutifully did.

We always found the club audiences in Lancashire were warm and friendly and, if they really liked the act, would applaud us again at the end of the evening as we left the building. In Yorkshire however, they were much tougher. The audiences there would stare, almost defying you to entertain them, it was hard going at the start of the show, but I'm happy to say we always won them around in the end.

In those days we had to travel over the Snake Pass to cross the Pennines, (before motorways) and this could be difficult in the winter. We went across one evening with light snow falling, but by the time we left the club after the gig, there was thick snow everywhere and we found the pass had been closed, so we had to find somewhere to stay. We came across an old Victorian hotel which had a night porter and was therefore still open and booked in. I can still remember Liz and I walking along a creeky corridor behind the elderly night porter who lead us to our room. As all the rooms had once been very large, they had been partitioned to make more smaller bedrooms, so the walls were quite thin. We didn't get much sleep that night as a man in the room next to ours, snored for England and drove us mad, although Liz and I always seemed to see the funny side of everything. To add insult to injury though, the hotel stay wiped out our profit for that night's gig.

As a rule we mostly agreed on song choice, but when Mary Hopkin had a big hit with a song called "Those Were The Days" and a couple of us wanted to perform it, Bill, who was a seriously good jazz musician, dug his heels in and refused to play it. In the end he reluctantly gave in having been outvoted, but just to appease him, we started to fool around in the number, putting a lot of goon like comedy into it and soon this combination of laughs and the rousing chorus became a big hit with audiences and we usually closed our show with it, leaving them shouting for "more".

Sadly there came a day when Lenny had to break the news to us that he would have to leave the act – a hard decision for him, but his family owned a big children's wear company and he was expected, as the eldest son, to help run the family business and he simply would not be able to devote the time to a professional group. We were very sorry to lose him, but were joined instead by yet another old friend of Johns - guitarist, Tom Muirhead and later by a terrific drummer called Steve Henshaw. Aside from the many enjoyable performances, I will always remember those two years with Les Bluesettes as a really happy time spent with a group of really talented young people who laughed a lot together despite occasionally having rows about material!

Most of the cabaret clubs in those days put on big shows as they were also casinos, and it was the casino takings which paid for the entertainment. That is until new legislation was brought in by the government which ruled that the casinos had to be separate businesses with separate entrances. Of course as the profits were made in the casinos, the result was that the entertainment side suffered as the clubs could no longer afford big live shows. Musicians and acts all found themselves with little or no work, where clubs had been open six nights per week, with six and seven piece bands and up to six acts on the bill, they went down to two or three nights, three musicians and one act and some closed altogether. Despite the Variety Artistes Federation, the Musicians Union and Equity organising marches on the streets, the government wouldn't back down and the entertainment industry suffered a huge blow.

Being self-contained, we fared better than many others, and eventually there came a time when Wilf and Steve thought they had taken us as far as they could as managers and they wanted to find a bigger management company to further our career. So they were thrilled for us when we were signed up by BDH Management who initially booked us in some good venues and also arranged for us to audition for Opportunity Knocks. We passed the audition and were booked to appear on the next series to be aired later that year. Things seemed to be going really well, then the agency said they wanted us to go out to Germany for three months to entertain on American bases. Bill had to buy a special case to carry his vibes and we paid for ferry tickets and various other expenses then, full of anticipation, we packed ourselves off and took our van across to Belgium on the ferry, before making the long drive to the first base in Germany.

When we met the club's entertainment director on the base, it became painfully obvious that a huge misunderstanding had occurred. We were an act, used to performing about an hour's musical cabaret spot and they were expecting a dance band to play 4 x 45 minute sets. How could this so-called top management agency get it so wrong? Nothing could be done, we had to turn around and return home, losing all the money we had spent on travel costs. On arrival back in the UK, the management took no responsibility, gave us no compensation, simply asked us to lay low for about three months as people in the business thought we were in Germany – this to protect their reputation rather than ours I suspect. Bill, the vibes player had by then been offered a place on the very first jazz course at a U.K.university and his wife was pregnant with their first child, so he decided to call it a day and the rest of us realised that without him, the unique sound we had worked so hard to achieve would not be the same any more. There are plenty of good guitarists, but top class vibraphone players are much harder to come by and even if we had found one, we had nothing to offer until the Opportunity Knocks series began again.

Sadly that was the end of Les Bluesettes.

Liz went on to form a double act with John, initially moving in with his family (and later marrying him). The rest of us went our separate ways. I have often wondered what might have been… if the American bases disaster hadn't happened and we had performed on *Opportunity Knocks* and maybe won… who knows? Could have been famous…

I was immediately invited to join a rock n'roll tribute show, they really wanted me for some reason, but I didn't feel that was right for me and I foolishly turned them down, thinking I would soon be with another act, I learned a valuable lesson from that… it would be six months before I sang professionally again.

I went to live in Bristol for a while with some good friends. Originally I had gone on a visit, but we went out one night and saw a really good band in a nice residency down there with two girl singers and I heard a rumour that one of them was leaving, so I ended up staying for a few weeks, working as a temporary secretary during the day in order to pay my friends some rent, and sure enough it was eventually announced that one girl singer was moving on and I auditioned. The two girls had very different voices, one sounded rather like me and the other was more soulful. Sadly for me it turned out to be the soul singer who was leaving. The band leader told me that had it been the other way around, he would have offered me the job, but he needed the two distinctly different voices to cover various hits... I was getting used to disappointment by then, but I never like to give up, so I decided to go to London, thinking I might have more luck. An old friend found me a bedsit in East Finchley as he knew the landlady and I signed on with another secretarial temp agency, so I could pay the rent whilst scouring the Stage newspaper each week for possible jobs and auditions.

Chapter 3
MATRIX

One day I auditioned for a London agency with the incongruous name Penny Farthing, that specialised in sending bands out to the American bases (ironically), in Germany, Italy and Turkey and as all groups were expected to have at least one female in the line up, which not all of them had, this agency would try to match female singers with all-male bands for these tours. The agent seemed to like me and was pleased with my singing. So things looked hopeful and sure enough it was not long before he telephoned me and told me he thought he had a suitable band for me to try out with. Hence I met up with David, Viv, Nick and Bert, known collectively as "Matrix". They were excellent musicians, intelligent and humorous guys, very much a blues based band who had also been writing their own material which they wanted to perfect whilst they were away on the bases. They hadn't really planned to have a girl band member and were a bit dubious about it at first, but as we got to know each other we hit it off. We rehearsed at their rented house in Chiswick and I remember sitting with them after practice watching the new comedy series on T.V. "Monty Python's Flying Circus", it seemed we already shared a quirky sense of humour. Vivien, the keyboards player and Bert the drummer (who was the son of the leader of the Dutch Swing College Band, Peter Schilperoort) were both ex-teachers, while David, lead guitar and flute and Nick, bass and double bass, were pro musicians who had known each other since childhood, The tour of bases was to be in Turkey and turned out to be one of the most interesting experiences of my life.

We left England on a chilly January day in a van affectionately known as "Specky" – I can't remember why. The electrical equipment and guitars were packed inside with the five of us and the drum kit and double base were strapped on the roof in waterproof covers. We went to Europe by ferry to Belgium and travelled through various countries including Austria, Yugoslavia (as it was called in 1971) and Bulgaria, then right across Turkey to the town of Diyarbakir (originally the capital of Armenia) on the eastern side of Turkey.

The journey took almost a week and we stayed in hotels on alternate nights and slept in the van in between. The guys were rather worried about suggesting this as they thought a girl would cause a fuss, but I thought it was a good idea, saving us all money. It seems they had been talking among themselves and come to the conclusion that for me to travel in a van halfway across the world with a bunch of guys I hardly knew meant I was either very brave and adventurous or completely nuts. I told them to let me know when they had decided. I never did find out. The journey was fascinating, despite discomforts, one of which was taking the main highway through Yugoslavia, which felt more like a dirt track in those days. The road was better in Bulgaria, but the towns seemed to me colourless places, apart from the gigantic red posters everywhere depicting happy workers (which seemed to contradict the miserable looks on most people's faces, I thought). Ordering meals in restaurants was a challenge as no-one spoke English and the Bulgarian alphabet was so different to ours we couldn't even make a guess as to what was on the menu. In one establishment Bert spent five minutes entertaining us and the other diners by doing an impersonation of a chicken, hoping they would bring him a chicken dish, but all he got was a bowl of soup with a raw egg dropped in. The rest of us took the easy option of pointing at another diner's bowl of pasta to convey our order to the waiter.

When we arrived at the Turkish border, the border guards decided to search our van thoroughly and roughly, so roughly they knocked Nick's beloved double bass off the roof and broke it. I thought Nick was going to cry. The customs men didn't care though and it would have been pointless and probably dangerous to argue with them. After searching the van thoroughly and finding nothing, they told us to pack everything again and let us through.

Our journey across Turkey to Diyarbakir was to take us across mountains, through marshy areas full of toads and tortoises and other varied and truly amazing scenery. One evening when we had been driving in a very remote part of the country and seen no-one for miles, we pulled into a lonely petrol station. The owner appeared and was thrilled to have customers and even more fascinated by the fact that we were a band of musicians. He insisted upon taking us into his home to meet his wives, parents and children. The house was one very large square room with tiles on the walls and what appeared to be wide shelves around the sides with bedrolls on them - these shelves evidently doubled up as their beds at night. The women were wearing traditional Turkish clothes and were all touching and admiring the red trouser suit I was wearing. We sat in a circle with them and the women deftly peeled fruit and passed it to us. None of them spoke English, but the garage owner had ascertained that we were a band on our way to the Americans to play and sing. They implored us to sing for them. A guitar was brought in from the van and Bert upturned a bucket to play as a drum. We sang them a song and the garage owner then wound up an ancient telephone on the wall and proceeded to shout excitedly into it, apparently inviting his brother to come over with his family and join in the party. In the meantime a bottle of Raki was opened – I have never been much of a drinker and at the time had no idea what Raki was, but seeing the women top the glasses up with water, thought it would be fairly weak. The glasses were passed around along with more slices of peeled oranges and other fruit. Then through the window we saw a sight which put me in mind of the Clampit family in the T.V. series the Beverley Hillbillies – it was a rickety truck, loaded up with people of all ages - the brother had arrived with his wives, his children and a very ancient couple – great grandparents I assumed. Introductions were made, more songs were sung, more raki was drunk and after my glass had been refilled for the fifth time I was well away and decided to teach these nice friendly Turkish folk how to do the Hokey Cokey – which they thought was wonderful, making a circle and trying to join in the words and doing all the actions with me – didn't do much for my rock'n'roll street cred, but I was by then on a roll and beyond caring – we were all having great fun. The band member who was driving, fortunately was still sober enough to call a halt and remind us all

11

that we should be on our way. We hugged our beaming hosts like old friends and thanked them for their hospitality before walking outside. As the night air hit me I realised just how unsteady I was and had to be helped back into the van by the boys. Ten minutes along the road they had to stop the van as I felt extremely queasy and, as I parted company with all the fruit and everything else I had eaten that day, by the side of the road, I apologised to David who was holding on to me – "I promise I am not normally like this" I said, David slapped me heartily on the back and said "Don't worry, you're one of the boys now" – a sentiment that was backed up by the rest of the band who had apparently thoroughly enjoyed watching me make a complete fool of myself for the past hour.

We eventually arrived at the base, which was "men only" and civilians, especially women, could not sleep there, so we were to stay in the "tourist" hotel in the town and travel in by the bus which collected workers who were employed on the base.

The hotel turned out to be pretty dreadful, all the rooms had en suite bathrooms with western style toilets, which is apparently why it was classed as "tourist", but they were really dirty and depressing. However, we were told that we would be able to eat our meals in the restaurant on the base, which meant we could have imported American food at rock bottom prices. The base restaurant staff were all Turkish and the head waiter, on hearing our complaints about the tourist hotel, asked us if we would like to meet his cousin who owned a really good, clean Turkish hotel in the town. We agreed and the following day we were taken to see the place. He was right about the cleanliness, the toilets were Eastern style of course (a hole in the floor with foot rests) and the showers were wet rooms, but the place was sparkling clean, the bedding was crispy white and the hotel was run with obvious pride – so we happily switched hotels, deciding on clean, germ-free nights over filthy bathrooms with sit-on loos. After all, apart from lying in bed until around noon, due to our long night's work (we performed four sets every night and five on a Saturday), we figured most of our time would be spent on the base anyway. The other problem we encountered in town was that in those days the sight of four long haired European guys and a single red haired young woman was found so fascinating by the locals that every day, as we waited for the bus in the town square, a huge crowd would gather and just stare at us. I had been advised to cover myself up, including my hair and did so, but the staring became quite intimidating sometimes, especially if the crowd grew large.

On our first night we worked to a mixed crowd of black and white servicemen who sat at separate tables to each other and for the most part, did not interact. Our first set was pretty light stuff, popular music which featured my singing a lot. The next set was a bit bluesier, the third funkier, louder and bluesier still and the last set gave me a rest as the band mostly played there own compositions which were more in the style of Led Zeppelin and sometimes a single piece would go on for eight to ten minutes.

Due to the overall blues based sound of the band, we unintentionally became a big hit with the black soldiers in particular and also minority of the white guys, but the white soldiers from the southern states, who preferred country-style music and were known as 'rednecks', did not care for us at all and at first would sit playing cards and raising their voices right in front of us. This caused the black soldiers who really liked us to start arriving early and grab the front tables so this couldn't happen any more. About a week after we arrived, one evening a huge black man walked in, a serious determined expression on his face and as he strode over to the bandstand, I felt the boys flinch. He looked very intimidating.

"Green Onions" was all he said as he stared at Nick who was centre stage. Nick looked at Viv who played keyboards, hoping that he would be able to play the Booker 'T' hit. Viv nodded vigorously and shouted out the key, launching into a totally unrehearsed, but very good version of Green Onions. The next evening the huge soldier came in again and walked straight up to the bandstand and once more just said "Green Onions", the boys played it and from that evening on, the second he appeared in the room, the band would immediately play "Green Onions" without being asked. Another fan of ours was a radio disc jockey on the base known as "Soul Doctor" Andy. He often joined us on the bandstand for a couple of numbers. One day he asked me to record some jingles for his radio show – I had to speak in the sexiest voice I could muster and say lines like "Oh I like that Dr. Andy" which Andy planned to air as he played a new recording, fading the record out as my voice came in. The first time he played that particular recording he had a phone call at the station immediately with a G.I. screaming down the phone "I LIKE IT, I LIKE IT, I LIKE IT!!!" Things seemed to be going well, so we thought, but we didn't realise just how deep the racial tensions were.

One evening we were told there was to be a special surprise party as one our regular fans was celebrating his birthday. He was a quiet and pleasant man who worked in the post office on the base – he also happened to be black. There was a strict rule that no dancing was allowed in the club, however, as it was a birthday celebration, I dedicated a song to the soldier for his birthday and stepped down from the stage and had a very short dance with him in front of the bandstand during the middle eight bars of the song – blink, and you could have missed it. Everyone cheered and I stepped back on to the stand and carried on with the song. Apart from singing "Happy Birthday" when a cake appeared, the rest of the evening was just like any other. But someone didn't like it…

…the next day, on our arrival at the base I was sent for by the sergeant in charge of the club and restaurant. He informed me, in his Southern drawl, that the band would no longer be able to use the laundry facilities on the base and, as the restaurant would be closing for a few days for refurbishment, we would only be able to buy sandwiches or would have to eat in town. I was of course, then admonished for dancing with a soldier, whilst being assured that it was nothing to do with the colour of his skin – some of his best friends were black – he added. Despite me defending myself by saying I wasn't dancing in the accepted sense of the rules, merely taking an eight bar twirl around the floor with the Birthday boy and then getting on with the rest of the night's performance and that it was obvious to everyone that nothing was meant or could be taken amiss by it, he wasn't to be moved – he had others to appease - and I left his office, feeling really bad that I would have to tell the boys we were to be punished by losing food and laundry facilities. I walked straight into a sea of angry black faces in the corridor outside his office, demanding to know what he said to me. This wasn't a small committee with a minor grievance, there was real menace in the air. I'm an honest person but, in that moment I knew that one wrong word from me and all hell could break loose. So I lied – "He was just explaining to me that the restaurant is closing for a few days, everything is fine."

"You sure? You sure he didn't tell you off 'bout dancin' with a black man last night, you ain't lyin' are you?"

"No. really it's fine". The "grilling" went on for several minutes, but I stuck to my guns and they had to just accept what I said and disperse, but the words "ticking" and "time bomb" came into my mind.

Two days later as I sat with the band eating yet another sandwich for "dinner" in the club, I was suddenly overwhelmed with sadness at the thought of the hatred that could make men behave that way. That we were being punished because of their hideous racial discrimination and I found this example of man's inhumanity to man deeply upsetting. I suddenly burst into floods of tears, unquenchable tears, I was racked with sobbing, it wouldn't stop and I couldn't speak to explain myself. Then a black soldier I had never seen before in my life ran over to the table, begging me to please stop crying, he couldn't bear to see me cry like that he said and were the band having money troubles? – if so he could give us some money to tide us over, if I would just stop crying. That made me feel even worse – how could I say "I'm crying for what you have to put up with and you're offering help to ME"? At that point, Bert leapt up from his seat and said "That's it! I am not seeing Carole cry like this – I'm going to see the base commander" and off he went. The boys, bless them, seemed to think I was crying simply because the restaurant and laundry facilities had stopped, and I was too choked up to explain. But some good came out of this situation and Bert's heroic stand, because the base commander said we could eat in the troop's canteen until the restaurant re-opened (and that we should have been told that by the sergeant in the first place) and the laundry was suddenly back at our disposal.

My other problems at Diyarbakir as the only western woman, were having nowhere to buy personal 'items' and finding a ladies' hairdresser. Eventually I decided my only hope for a haircut was to go to the barber on the base. He was also Turkish and didn't understand English so I could only mime that I wanted a haircut. He grinned and nodded and I sat in the chair, he then picked up his scissors, pulled a handful of my hair above my head and cut it off in one snip. I leapt out of the chair, thanked him, threw some coins at him and ran out before he could do any more harm. I was left with something resembling a badly styled mullet. Fortunately my hair grows quickly and I did have a wig (they were fashionable at that time) that I could wear on stage until the worst grew out.

The few weeks spent at Diyarbakir provided a mix of emotional highs and lows, meeting some good friends and happy music making, but also some very ugly insights into human behaviour. Little did I know that I would be back the following year and would see a different but equally disturbing situation.

We were on the road again, this time to the coastal town of Sinop and during late March and April, this lovely town offered sunny weather, seaside, normal clothes, a base where wives were allowed into the restaurant and club, and where U.S. missiles were pointed across the Black Sea towards Russia.

The atmosphere at Sinop was entirely different. The serving men were mostly from the air force and navy and, as there were missiles there, quite a lot of them were very bright guys with specialist training and knowledge. Some of the men had their wives and families with them, not living on the actual base, but renting houses in the town, so it was great for me have the company of some other women. Although Sinop was a more modern place than Diyarbakir, there were still some laws which had to be followed. The hotel where we stayed would post a guard at the end of the corridor as I was a single woman, to make sure no males entered my room. As there were no telephones in the rooms this made communication with the rest of the band a bit difficult, so we told them that David - who was of similar colouring to myself, fair with blue eyes basically – was my brother, amazingly they believed us and David was able to come to my room without fear of being arrested or falling whilst climbing up on to the balcony, which is how they had communicated with me during the first couple of days!

However I did get a knock at my door around 11am on the 10th April and found a couple of sergeants from the base holding a bunch of flowers and wishing me a happy birthday, they told me to hurry up and get dressed as the band were waiting downstairs and we were all going out for a steak and champagne breakfast! I got presents too - it was a lovely surprise.

The shows were really successful at Sinop, we seemed to appeal to everyone there. I did notice, though, that people in the audience didn't drink much alcohol, mostly cola, but by the last set when the boys played their own stuff, the majority seemed to be in a trance. It wasn't long before we realised the place was awash with drugs. Mostly marijuana, speed and acid, it was rife. It would be nice to think the deliriously happy expressions on the faces in the crowd were down to our singing and playing alone, but when half your audience is almost always stoned, it can be hard to tell. At the end of the night, people would often come up to me, shake my hand and say "great show" and stuck in my palm would be silver foil containing something we could get high on. Trouble was, we couldn't tell what we'd been given, so it usually got flushed down the toilet.

Not always though, one day we all went for a huge party on the beach, there was a great deal of frisbee throwing (as we had never encountered frisbees before, we thought they were great) and for the first time in my life, I took some 'speed'. It wasn't long before I found myself running up and down the beach unable to burn up all the energy I suddenly had and I also happily ate an entire loaf of bread by myself whilst sitting in the sand. At some point an old Turkish man came along on horseback and after taking his picture, I was allowed to ride his horse on the beach. In the evening when we were back at the base club, we performed the usual four or five sets. Having burned up so much energy I should have slept well that night, but instead stayed awake for a further 24 hours – the speed must have been powerful stuff and I vowed then to make it my first and last, as I can get pretty cross when I don't sleep.

Having the company of other women again was nice though and one day, we girls decided to go the ancient Turkish bath house in town on "women's day" – the baths were open for men six days per week and for women on one day! We all stripped off in the ancient steam rooms, except for our pants which we were not allowed to remove. Presently a door opened, and we stared in trepidation at the gruesome sight of a very large, ugly woman with a towel wrapped around her huge bulk, brandishing some sort of rough scouring cloth and heading meaningfully in our direction. She was the sort of woman who appeared to make the ground shake as she walked. This vision then proceeded to "scour" each one of us down until our skins were bright red. By the time we left some three hours later, we were squeaky clean, invigorated (not to mention slightly raw) and had rather aching heads after three hours in the hot steamy atmosphere. Interesting definitely, but on the whole not an experience I would like to repeat.

What was a treat for the boys and me was being taken out for a trip on a boat around the bay by Captain Ahbesh, a local fisherman we had met, who then took us to his house where we shared the most delicious fish soup with his family. It was a lovely day and great to meet a Turkish family in their home.

On one of our nights off we went to the base cinema and watched the brand new movie 'Easy Rider' which later became a cult classic, but at the time had only just been released in the States. We were then invited back to the rooms of three airmen on the base – I had to walk in the middle of a tight group of people so I wouldn't be seen, as women were strictly forbidden in the sleeping quarters. It transpired that their three rooms were known as "The Bar", "The Restaurant" and "The Shop" as their cupboards were full to the brim with illicit military issue food, drink and other goods! So we had a very good party, courtesy of and unknown to the American Military.

On the whole we really enjoyed Sinop, but eventually our third month in Turkey came to an end.

We could have stayed in Turkey longer, but disaster struck when Bert the drummer developed pains in his wrist and did not want to risk playing drums, especially for the length of time required out there. I think there were also some doubts as to whether "Specky" would last much longer without needing serious money spending on it. So we set off once more on the long journey overland back to Belgium and the ferry home. We packed up Specky, having dumped any drugs given to us by "well wishers". On the way back we stopped in the mountains and watched the sunrise out of a star filled sky. It was a stunning sight.

When we reached the border, the customs officials, once again determined that we must be carrying drugs and took the van apart again, but once more finding nothing they eventually gave up their search and sent us on our way. "Well at least we knew they could not find any drugs, thank goodness we dumped it all" somebody said. "Well not quite all" said David "I put some LSD in the in the back of the Les Paul". This was a shock to the rest of us, after the ferocity of the search we had just endured and having been told what the inside of Turkish prisons were like and that the key would be practically thrown away on westerners caught with drugs, we all really had a go at him.

The weather was much warmer on the journey back and when we reached Sofia, the capital of Bulgaria we decided to stay in a hotel for the night and do a little sightseeing. We went into the cathedral there which was awesome. We also noted that because of the communist state all restaurants had more or less the same menus with the same prices and that all the hotels, large and small were also the same price (very cheap). We stayed in a very grand and once supremely luxurious hotel. My room was vast, with huge pieces of ornate and beautifully carved furniture and an adjoining bathroom suite big enough to have a party in. It cost the equivalent of ten shillings (now 50p in today's money) in UK currency at the time. When we were going back to our rooms that night, we noticed that the other guests had all put their shoes outside their bedroom doors to be cleaned during the night. This was too much for the boys, who ran about putting them all outside different doors – we missed the fun though, as we left quite early the next morning.

Our next stop was Yugoslavia and we found a very beautiful and quiet spot in the countryside where we decided to try the LSD smuggled out by David. Only four of us took it, leaving Bert to keep an eye on us. Looking back, I can't think what he would have done if help were needed, medical or otherwise. I can't remember much about it except that everything I looked at seemed magnified and more beautiful and/or ugly as the case might be and that I could only be aware of one thing or sensation at a time, like a super high concentration, causing me to literally "hear the grass grow". I would add that was my FIRST and LAST acid trip, so I have nothing to compare it with.

I really enjoyed my time with the boys and we had some laughs, Bert frequently going into a rendition of "Old Father Thames" in various public places, with his rich deep bass/baritone voice. It was an emotional farewell with Matrix, we had shared some amazing experiences in a very short time and their dreams of becoming the next great band seemed to be dissolving as Bert's wrist problems might be serious and I think they split up. I had often wondered what happened to them all and where they are now. However, having recently heard about a highly acclaimed jazz saxophonist/drummer in the Cambridge area by the name of Bert Schilperoort, I googled his name and found him! We have had a wonderful long catch up on the phone and I now know that despite his tendinitis, he has once more been able to play drums again after a long break during which time he returned to teaching and learned to play the saxophone. He now plays jazz. I have also found out that Nick Stephens the bass player, continued to play and has become very well established in the avante-garde jazz world.

Following that trip I felt I was a changed person and knew it would be a long time before I could "settle down" to "everyday life", if ever. Although I never again took drugs of any kind, I did however get "hooked" on travel.

Chapter 4

P.J. PROBY

I returned home to Manchester where I'm sure my parents were very relieved to see me home safe and sound, and a short time later I received a telephone call that would send my life in show business off in another new direction.

I was having dinner at home when the telephone rang. It was the girl-friend of Tom "Smiley" Bowker (banjo and dobro player of note at the time). She asked me if I would help out, as the P.J. Proby Show was in Manchester and due to start a week long show at Fagin's Nightclub that night and one of his three girl backing singers had not turned up. Tom Bowker was playing in his backing band and we were old friends from the advertising agency. I agreed and went along and met the rest of the band and the other two backing singers, one black girl and one white.. I spent no more than an hour running through the basic vocals for the act, before being thrown in the deep end. Singing and winging it for his first evening's performance. The show went well fortunately, so when I turned up the following evening I expected a fairly smooth time – not to be. More panic – the other white backing singer had absconded with the fiddle player. That left Selena and myself as the only two backing vocalists. The trouble was that Jim Proby performed a "country style" dance in the middle of the show with one of the girls, but he had a prob-lem with black people (something apparently, so I was informed, to do with growing up on a plantation and finding a black man in bed with his mother) and would therefore not dance with Selena. "But I don't know the routine" I said to the band, to no avail, "when he turns around to grab one of you to dance with, he will pick you because you're white" was all I received as a reply. Sure enough, that's what happened. I just had to keep smiling and second guessing what was coming next, but he seemed happy and somehow we got away with it.

Selena and I were chatting before the show, she told me she had recently left the cast of the musical Hair and was doing the backing singing as a fill in while looking for something else. She also complained about the poor accommodation she had been given in Manchester, so the next day I asked my parents if she could come and stay with us at home. They agreed, though I hadn't realised how strange they found it as she was the first black person they had ever met or invited into their home. But when they met her they thought she was lovely and she stayed with us for the rest of the week - well almost.

Things went 'belly up' on the Thursday evening. The club was packed and the owner was sitting out front with his wife and family, when Jim Proby came on it was obvious that he was either drunk or stoned (probably both), I even had to walk forward and switch his microphone on for him as this task was evidently beyond him. His hitherto really good performance took a complete nose dive and as the audience picked up on his state and began to react, he told them they could "f**k themselves. Needless to say, that was his last night at Fagins.

The following day when Selena and I went to collect our pay, sadly only for five days instead of seven, the agent who booked for the club told us that he thought we were the best part of the show and that if we ever decided to form an act to get in touch with him. Selena went back to London, but we decided to keep in touch.

A few weeks later I was called by man who had been brave (or rash) enough, to take over management of P.J.Proby and wanted me to sing backing vocals for him again in a nightclub in Preston, Lancashire for a week, along with Selena. "All his problems are sorted out" he said, "it will never happen again." Call me a cynic, but I agreed ONLY on condition that I would be guaranteed to get a full week's pay even if JP was "paid off" for any reason.

So I met up with Selena again and for the first four shows everything was perfect, then on the fifth night, on came Jim Proby in exactly the same condition he had got himself into at Fagin's.

This time he decided to have a racist rant on stage against black people and Selena stood behind him with her fist in the air in the black panther salute of the time. Despite his drunken/high state, the club decided the young black girl standing behind him, listening to his dreadful remarks was at fault for making the sign and should be asked to leave the stage.

He was, however paid off yet again. By then Selena and I had ideas of our own about possibly forming a vocal duo, but were not sure just how we would be able to do it, with me living in Manchester and Selena in London.

As chance would have it a couple of weeks later I saw an ad. in the Manchester Evening News for two girl singers to front a band at a new venue in Denton, Greater Manchester. I telephoned the owner and asked whether he would have any problems with a black girl and a white girl (things were sooo different back then and the situation at Diyarbakir had made me more aware of this). He said he wouldn't have any problem, so I called Selena and told her about it. She decided to come up to Manchester and we auditioned successfully for the club and Selena moved in with my family on a more permanent basis while we rehearsed and worked at the club, all the time using our residency wages to pay for putting our own act together and paying for music and costumes. There was however, a male singer with the band already and it wasn't long before we realised that he was not happy at sharing the limelight with two attractive young women who were getting a lot of attention. He sometimes made snide remarks, creating a bit of an atmosphere, then one day the owner asked Selena and I into his office to explain why we hadn't been coming to band practice. "The band leader hasn't called any rehearsals recently" was our reply. It transpired that the male vocalist who had been given the task of giving us practice times just hadn't bothered to tell us, making it look as though we were at fault. We were livid. The owner, was a really nice man and he realised what was going on and wanted us to stay, but there was now an unpleasant atmosphere and as we had been putting our own act together we decided that we didn't have to put up with it any longer, and resigned anyway. My mum secretly arranged for two enormous bouquets of flowers to be awarded to us on stage on our last night at the club and the male vocalist had to grit his teeth into a smile and present them to each of us, wishing us luck whilst the audience enthusiastically applauded. No-one knew who had sent them, we had assumed they were from the management at the time, as did everyone else. Bless my lovely mum.

Chapter 5
CONTRAST

When we felt we had enough material and costumes for a show of our own we went back to the agent who had advised us to get together and auditioned for him and he started to get bookings for us. We called ourselves "Contrast".

There was no such thing as political correctness then and, as the sight of a black and a white girl singing together at that time was a bit novel for some, to say the least, when we went on stage I would say "Good evening" followed by a bit of opening jargon, then Selena would step forward and repeat what I had just said word for word. I would say "I just said all that Selena" and she would reply "Well, now they've got it in black and white". This makes me cringe now, but at the time, it got a really big laugh, sometimes applause and always "broke the ice".

We got lots of bookings though and went all over UK, also appearing in Ireland and Malta. The Malta trip was actually a Christmas/new year Thomson holiday at the Mellieha Bay Hotel. The deal was that we travelled over on the package holiday in return for four cabaret shows over Christmas and New Year's eve. Two families who were on the same package holiday really liked us and we even sat with them at mealtimes as we got on so well. Although it was December, the weather was excellent and we spent Boxing Day around the hotel pool. We also visited the neighbouring island of Gozo. Despite there being no fee, we had to admit we had a great holiday.

There were changes in Malta after we left, including some rioting as Dom Mintoff , their Prime Minister, who had always wanted Malta to be free of British rule and influence was stirring up trouble there, finally getting his way in 1974 including the end of British sterling as their currency.

Another oversees trip took us on a tour of American bases in Turkey and Italy, where we were part of a show comprising comedian Jerry Harris, a blonde belly dancer called Layla and ourselves, but although we had musical parts for a four piece band, the agent only sent a pianist with us for the Turkish part of the tour, which, as we did all pop music, sounded pretty naff. By a strange coincidence we found ourselves back at the base in Diyarbakir exactly one year on and boy, how things had changed.

The personnel on the base were by then mostly black and they were allowed to have wives and families with them. So when Selena and I went on stage we got a rather hostile reception, from the black women in particular, and during the interval a couple of black soldiers came round backstage, pushed Selena back against the wall and remonstrated with her for working with a white girl! The pendulum had swung the opposite way with a vengeance and I was firmly shown the other side of the coin.

On this tour we visited three or four bases around Turkey and spent time in the capital Ankara and Istanbul. Ankara was modern and seemingly more "westernised" than the other towns, however an incident at the main hospital has always stayed in my mind as a reminder of how different reality can be to how things seem.

The belly dancer had a slight accident when she slipped in the shower and banged her big toe on the pipework – not amusing when you dance for a living. The hotel manager who spoke good English offered to take her to the hospital and I went with her for support. She went off to be "looked at" and have her toes x-rayed. She was gone quite a while and told me later that no less than four doctors had come in turn to "sound her chest" with their stethoscopes, which was quite unusual for someone with a toe injury, but then she also had a 40 DD bust measurement which I think may have had something to do with it.

During this time I sat in the waiting area with the hotel manager and was fascinated by the sight of a peasant couple sitting opposite. The woman was obviously in pain and sat, rocking backwards and forwards, with her feet on the seat and knees up to her chin as I don't think she was used to chairs. Her skin was very brown and she wore many beads and small coin-like droplets around her head and neck. Her distressed husband in his peasant outfit of shabby grey suit and flat cap, was pleading with doctors and anyone who would listen, but I could not understand what was being said so asked the hotel manager what the matter was. He told me the man was pleading with the doctors, saying that he had walked many many miles to reach the hospital in Ankara, supporting his wife as she was injured in some way and in extreme pain and needed X-rays, but the doctors would not treat her because he had little or no money. She wept the whole time. My heart went out to them, I felt so helpless and would have paid their bill if I had had enough money, but I didn't. It was so, so sad and deeply frustrating. If I had been able to speak Turkish, I would have really caused a fuss, maybe tried to organise a whip round, but other cultures can be so hard to reach or understand. The same doctors who had time to waste sounding the chest of a big breasted blonde with an injured toe, had no time or compassion for a poor couple who had walked for miles in the hope of pain relief and help, and no-one else seemed in the least bit interested. I have no idea what happened to the woman after we left the hospital, I hope someone took pity on them.

After we left Turkey, the show moved on to Italy, we had to travel there by train for some reason and the tour's road manager Ken met up with us again there. By the time we arrived in Italy we had become friendly with our Italian fellow passengers in the carriage, even being shown photos of people's children, and had told them where we were headed and why. Thank goodness, because when we drew into a major station and we had dozed off, a young Italian man in the carriage began shouting and waking us up because he had heard an announcement about changing trains and knew we should be getting off and going to another platform. This lovely guy then helped us with our bags across to the right platform for our connecting train, averting a possible disaster.

It was in Southern Italy that the tour took a turn for the better and the highlight for Selena and I was our appearance at the Pink Flamingo Club in Naples, which was packed with American sailors as two U.S.

Naval vessels were in port. The club had a really good English house band, who could read music well. This band played our arrangements brilliantly and we went down a storm. The audience were clapping, whistling and cheering and when our spot was over they wouldn't let us off until we sang "You've Lost that Loving Feeling" again as an encore. It was definitely the best night of our tour and restored our faith in ourselves as an act.

When we were in Northern Italy, I said I would like to go to Venice and buy a small piece of Venetian glass for my mum as I always tried to take her a glass object from the places I visited. The young manager of the new hotel where we were staying said his father also owned a hotel in Venice and if I could get there, his father could arrange for me to visit a factory and see the glass being made. So the road manager Ken offered to drive me there and it was all arranged. We called in briefly at Pisa on the way to see the leaning tower, then went on to Venice to the factory address I had been given. What the manager had not told me was that his father owned the best hotel in Venice and that he had personally asked the glass factory owner to show me around the factory as a special favour and I wished to purchase something. This unnerved me and I hoped he wasn't expecting someone wealthy who was going to buy half a dozen chandeliers as I only wanted one glass. Ken and I were taken on a lovely personal tour, having everything explained to us about the history and methods of making the glass, and when we at last reached the shop, I bought a single amethyst wine glass (which I was informed was the best) and thanked them most gratefully before taking my leave, feeling more than slightly embarrassed at my humble purchase.

Back in the UK, we went to Harrogate, Yorkshire to appear in cabaret for a week. Whilst there Selena and I decided we must have afternoon tea at Betty's Tea Rooms. I think we caused a bit of a stir though. When we entered the tea room we noticed that almost all the tables were taken by respectable looking middle aged ladies, wearing hats. Whereas, being the early '70's I had on the latest fashion of plaid trousers and a bright yellow jacket and Selena was wearing beige leather trousers and a floor length leopard print fur waistcoat. We could sense all eyes upon us, but we still enjoyed the cakes.

A week spent in Scotland appearing at Rangers supporters club in Glasgow, was fantastic. We were a little nervous when we found we were following Lulu who had appeared the previous week, but the superb house band comprised members of the Scottish radio orchestra and made us sound great. It was a beautiful cabaret room and the show could also be seen by members in the club's lounge viewed on monitor screens which were suspended over the tables. It was one of the most luxurious clubs we performed in and we enjoyed the week in Glasgow very much.

Ireland provided us with great gigs in Limerick and Dublin which we also really enjoyed, apart from the digs where we stayed in Dublin, the landlady there would put our breakfast on the table (a single rasher of bacon and one egg each) and then call upstairs to wake us up, so our food would be cold when we got to it. She had no understanding of the timetables of artistes who needed to be on top form and at peak energy in the evening, and so needing a lie-in in the morning. However everyone else we had dealings with there were really friendly and hospitable. We did however encounter a problem with the flight home. Selena and I were the only two passengers apparently booked on an Aer Lingus flight from the States which was landing in Dublin to drop off and collect passengers before continuing to the UK. We checked in fine, the flight was called and we went to the correct gate to wait but no-one came to let us through, as time went on we found a representative of Aer Lingus and told them, but were assured someone would come to take our boarding cards and open the gate. We went twice more to the Aer Lingus desk to report that no-one had come to the gate, but were again told there was no problem. Still nobody came and as we could actually see the plane through the window, we then watched it take off with our luggage but sadly without us. Annoyingly we then had to wait about four more hours for another flight.

We also went out to troubled Northern Ireland which was becoming a dangerous place then, with the threat of bombings on the increase, in fact when we were shown up to our room in the Europa Hotel, the windows were just being put back in by glaziers after a vehicle bomb blast earlier in the week. The hotel front now had huge concrete containers filled with flowers situated in front of the hotel to prevent anyone from driving up and parking outside.

In Belfast, we worked at the Abercorn club. We got used to having to go through checkpoints and having our bags searched by British soldiers in the city. The shows however went well and on the final day, Saturday, we performed a show at lunchtime as well as in the evening, flying back to the UK the next morning. Meanwhile another act arrived to take over, David Copperfield, who went on to do the lunchtime show on the following Saturday 4th March 1972 and that was the day a bomb was detonated in the restaurant crowded with shoppers, mostly women with children, below the Abercorn club in which two young women died and 130 people were horrifically injured, many losing their limbs. So it fell to David Copperfield to keep the upstairs audience calm and help guide them out of the club away from the carnage beneath. One week earlier it would have been us. A sobering thought, I often wondered how we would have coped.

Whenever we worked in the London area we always stayed at Selena's parents home with her brother, her older married sister whose husband was in Nigeria and her sister's two gorgeous children. I always enjoyed staying with them and eating a bit of her mum's "soul food". One day we were asked to go to London by Selena's previous agent there to audition for Cliff Richard's next T.V. series as backing singers. The agent said the producers were looking for three black girls really, but we thought if we asked another friend of Selena's who was Mauritian, to join us they might go for the idea of a group of mixed nationalities. And that is exactly what happened - but not for us. All the other three girl groups at the audition were black, we were the only group of mixed race and while we sang our number on stage, someone stole my handbag. The building was searched and it was eventually found in the ladies toilets, minus my purse, which, apart from my money, contained both our train tickets back to Manchester. To add insult to injury, when the new Cliff Richard series was shown on T.V. his new backing group were three girls of different nationalities – one black, one white, one oriental. Wonder where they got that idea?

Selena and I worked together for about eighteen months in total, but somewhere along the way our friendship soured, I still don't know why, but Selena began a relationship with a young man who lodged with my parents and became really bitchy towards me and the atmosphere was strained to say the least, so we decided to call it a day and go our separate ways, but carry on until the shows that were already booked in were completed, which was a mistake when I look back, because the horrible situation really got to me. I became very depressed at that time and there were a couple of days when I didn't speak to anyone at all and felt almost suicidal, then a friend called me out of the blue (I later found that he was asked to by my mum) and took me out for a drink and a catch up. Somehow an evening of talking to an old friend seemed to break the spell and put me back together. I was able to pull myself together after that and am pleased to say have never felt that way since.

I started to scour the ads in The Stage newspaper again and saw one looking for a girl singer to join a group based in the North East. I answered it and found myself travelling up to Middlesbrough to audition for a band called Scarlet. When I arrived I met a duo I had worked with before on the circuit and one of them offered to play guitar for me at the audition which was helpful. After returning to Manchester, I received a call from the band leader asking me to join the group.

Chapter 6
SCARLET

I wasn't sure about singing with another band, as I really preferred performing in theatres and cabaret, but jobs were scarce and, having turned that offer down with the rock and roll show after Les Bluesettes disbanded, I had learned my lesson, besides I wanted to sing again. So when I was asked, despite having to move up to Middlesbrough, I accepted and soon found myself a house share with three other young women who were all librarians. Needless to say, I never saw much of my house mates as they worked during the day and I worked at night in clubs in the North East. It was there that on days we weren't rehearsing, I read the whole of The Lord of the Rings trilogy during the afternoons, usually accompanied by the music of Led Zeppelin and the Moody Blues on the Hi-Fi.

Strangely there was only one Geordie in the band, the other three members were from Somerset and Wiltshire, so I'm not quite sure how they came to be based up there. We performed lots of local gigs in the North East, but it wasn't long before we were booked to go out to American bases in Germany again. I was able to advise the band, who had not been before that we would need to travel by ferry to Belgium, not France as we would need a carnet (a document listing our equipment and values to enable free transport of goods in another country). For some reason, the leader of the group Keith seemed to think this was tosh and ignored my advice, instead booking the ferry to Calais. On arrival in France we were pulled over by customs and asked to produce our carnet or deposit £2,000 with them until our return trip. On that occasion I was sorry to be proved right, but resisted saying "I told you so" and we returned on the next ferry to Dover, rebooking a crossing to Belgium where they didn't demand carnets, with all the extra time and expense that entailed. Keith did not like to be proved wrong, so the atmosphere was a bit weird for a while.

However we all cheered up on reaching our destination - a truly beautiful ski resort called Garmische-Partenkirchen in Bavaria. We were to be the house band in one of two hotels used for US military personnel to spend some R and R, for the first month. After which we would be touring various bases in Germany and the third month, although we didn't know it at the time, would return (by popular request, which was very pleasing) to the hotel in Garmische once again. During that first month in Garmische, there was thick snow everywhere and people had built snow sculptures in the town. Although we did not ski, I used to go ice skating in the Olympic style ice stadium there which had both indoor and outdoor rinks where you could skate from one rink to the other without ever leaving the ice. It was fun during the annual Fasching celebrations to see the local children skating in fancy dress and all sorts of other crazy stunts going on in the town.

It was a lovely place, although the air was very dry which caused me (as a redhead), to become full of static electricity, so I kept getting minor shocks from anything metal. The keyboard player had the same problem and one day he passed the van key to me and sparks flew giving us both a shock.

Because of the Vietnam war, and the constant threat to the young men in our audiences of getting their papers to send them out there, the peace sign was very much in use at that time and at the end of every performance, when the audience was cheering and clapping, I always held up both arms and gave the sign for peace which got an enthusiastic response every time. The conscripts in American forces at the time were given a choice (if they were up to the standard) of two years in the army or four years in the air force. They came from all backgrounds and everyone from shoe shine boys to university graduates were enlisted, so it was fascinating talking to them and finding out their different stories and views on their situation. What most of them had in common though was an absolute dread of getting the orders to go to Vietnam.

On our return visit to Garmische, the snow had melted and given way to green hills and spring flowers. It was so scenically beautiful I felt I should be running about the hills singing "The Sound of Music" like Maria Von Trapp, and the air was so clear that when we returned to England and drove through London, I could actually see the dirt in the city air around us. I went one day with a friend on a trip to Oberammergau, famous for its Passion Play and also for its wonderful wood carving which I particularly enjoyed seeing and we also visited Neuschswanstein Castle, built by Ludwig II who, in doing so, almost bankrupted the treasury and where Wagner had been a frequent guest.

I got on well with the guys in the group except occasionally with the leader, Keith, who was a real chauvinist, we seemed to have a serious personality clash though it didn't matter most of the time as the rest of us were happy. Whilst there I became good friends with an Apache girl who sang with a band in another hotel, her name was Pasha Vashti and she was very beautiful and exotic, and another girl called Cherry who was a go-go dancer from the UK with a third band in the town. I suppose, as the only females with male groups, we felt a bond. During that month a guest cabaret came to the hotel in the form of the New Christie Minstrels, who were very good. Pasha told me she had once auditioned for them but was turned down for being too sexy looking for their all American "apple pie" image.

On the band's last night at Garmische, some of our fans decided to throw a big party for us at which they had made a large tub full of the drink known as a Harvey Wallbanger – Vodka, Orange Juice and Galliano. Not being much of a drinker I once again didn't realise the potency of this fruity delight and as it was such a fun party I drank what seemed like gallons of it throughout the evening. I recall being eventually helped back to my hotel room by the drummer from the other English band and giggling all the way across the hotel grounds.

The next morning when we were supposed to vacate our rooms in the hotel, I was glued to my bed with the mother of all hangovers. I felt so bad and when the Turkish chambermaid kept knocking on the door all I could say was "kranken" in a pathetic croak. Needless to say I have never touched a Harvey Wallbanger since.

Following this successful tour of Germany, we returned to the UK feeling very good about ourselves and the same agent, having had great reports of our shows, booked us into a hotel in Douglas, Isle of Man for a summer season. It was the summer of 1973.

We only worked a few weeks at the hotel. At the beginning of the season, there were no early customers, people came in around 9 pm onwards and we were officially supposed to play from 8 pm which we did at first, playing to the staff, until the manager told us not to bother going on until customers came in. Our keyboard player, who could be rather "off the wall"at times, made the mistake of getting into a shouting match one day with the hotel owner's wife, the rest of us had nothing to do with it and didn't even know what it was about, but the outcome was that she had her husband fire us on the grounds that we did not start playing on time (even though that had been agreed with the management). I was devastated, as I had never been dismissed from anywhere in my life and feeling that enough was enough, I refused to go back to England with the band. However, I knew I had to do something to pay my rent until the end of the season. A friend told me a photographic business in Douglas was looking for someone to complete a small team of photographers to take photos of holidaymakers enjoying places of entertainment and I thought "I like photography, I can do that". And so I did for a couple of weeks until one fateful evening when the boss asked me and another photographer David to go to the big entertainment complex on the sea front called Summerland as they were expecting bumper crowds that night. He told us to make sure we arrived there by 7.30 p.m. prompt.

David was supposed to pick me up before 7.30 p.m. but he didn't turn up until 7.45 p.m. and as we turned onto the seafront we were met by the sight of flames and billowing black smoke coming from Summerland and hundreds of sobbing people moving down the promenade en masse away from the inferno. My colleague was by profession a press photographer and he just leapt from the car and began to take photographs, on instinct I suppose. I was in shock, watching all these distressed people and overwhelmed by a sense of wanting to put my arms around them and comfort them all.

Fifty-one men, women and children died in that inferno, and many more were injured and badly traumatised. I knew some of the musicians and entertainers who worked there, one of whom, drummer Malcolm Ogden, perished. I had just started seeing a Dutch DJ who worked there and he shattered his kneecap when catching a baby that a terrified parent had thrown over the balcony to safety. He told me afterwards of the horrors inside, seeing the Oroglass literally melting and falling onto people, he said they looked as though their faces were melting. It was all made worse by the fact that some of the emergency doors were locked and no-one from the venue had called the fire brigade. Apparently the only calls to the fire brigade were from a passing taxi driver and a ship off shore. The fire was started by three teenage boys who had broken into the disused cigarette kiosk and thrown a lighted match away. People who worked there thought it was just a small fire that would soon be put out by extinguishers, so no-one bothered to organise people and try to get them out. Families visiting the place were split up with adults in one entertainment section and kids in different ones, but the fire spread so fast it took everyone by surprise and turned into the greatest tragedy in the Isle of Man's history, as family members ran about trying to find one another. There were many acts of heroism and kindness, but there were also terrible accusations and personal attacks blaming people. The architect who had designed the structure using Oroglass, which had melted with such horrific effects was back in Denmark and could not be contacted.. It was a truly horrendous incident and even though I was not inside the building when it happened it still had a profound effect on me for a long time. It was couple of weeks later when I got around to asking my colleague why he was late picking me up that night (possibly saving both our lives in the process) "I don't know" he said "just dawdling I suppose". I wrote a letter to my best friend Gillian back in Manchester and told her about it and how I felt and remember asking her to pass it around to certain other friends of mine as I knew I would only be able to write it once. My parents came over to the island to see me and I returned home with them, but I found it too difficult to talk about what happened even to them.

After a short break at home, I felt it was time to get back to my singing career and so started reading the ads in The Stage once more, eventually applying for an audition in London to join a newly forming act of one man and two girls to be called Trilogy.

I went down to London by train for the audition. I didn't realise that I would have to catch a train leaving just before the cheap day rate began in order to get there on time and had only taken a small amount of cash with me and back then did not possess a credit card. Faced with the choice of paying for a single ticket and making the audition on time or waiting for the next cheap day return and being too late, or simply returning home – I impulsively bought the single ticket and decided to worry about getting back later.

Some instinct told me it was the right move at the time. I met this young man called Robin Wyatt and a pianist who accompanied me singing the Beatles' song "Here, There and Everywhere". Then I waited in an adjoining room whilst Rob spoke with the pianist who I heard say "She's definitely the best one today". Rob reappeared and invited me for a coffee and explained his idea for the act and invited me to join. I asked him if he had any bookings in the offing for the act and he said "Not yet, but what are you doing at the moment?" I said "nothing" and, seeing his point, agreed to join Trilogy. He then asked if I had any further questions and that's when I asked him if he could loan me the train fare to get back to Manchester – he's never let me forget that.

Chapter 7
TRILOGY

Robin had recently returned from his second season on the QE2 as part of an act called the Bigwoods, but now wanted to form a new act along with two girl singers. He lived in Margate in Kent where he owned a small café which his older sister Jean managed for him, above which was a flat where he was able to accommodate myself and the other member of the new act, Linda, who was primarily a dancer and came from Cramlington in the North East. So we two northern girls, now found ourselves down south. My stage name was Carole Seton at the time and Linda called herself Lynne Lacey, Robin used his own name of Rob Wyatt. All three names were to change during the years we worked together, but that was how we began.

We spent some weeks working very hard rehearsing songs, having costumes made, photos taken and sending out publicity and by the spring of 1974 we were an established working act on the circuit of clubs in the UK and we also came to the attention of Combined Services Entertainment, the organisation that sends shows off to entertain British servicemen around the world. We did our first show for them in Belfast that year, it was to be the first of many. In fact we performed a total of twelve CSE tours in Northern Ireland over the years we were together. When the shows arrived in there, we would check into a hotel and then be taken by coach to the first venue of the day and perform for the troops, then onto a second venue, perform again and back to the hotel. The following day after breakfast we would board the coach and travel to another base for a late morning performance, followed by an afternoon gig at another,

New World Singers

The original line up of Les Bluesettes

The Starlettes

LES BLUESETTES

Les Bluesettes - final line up

Bert, Dave, Nik and Viv – Matrix

Me, with Dave and Matrix - Sinop, Turkey

Carole and Selena

Contrast - Carole and Selena in our wigs!

*Scarlet, at Villiers Hotel,
Isle of Man*

CSE show, Belfast

Carole and Linda by the Wailing Wall, Israel

In picturesque Stavanger, Norway

Trilogy

The Masira State Railway with Jimmy Marshall, Terry Light-foot and Chantelle

'Let's strike a pose', Jimmy said!
With Jimmy Edwards in Doha

With Ronnie Corbett, Bahrain Hilton

With Kenny Lynch and Jimmy Tarbuck

With Mike Reid and the Pools winner,
Caesar's Palace, Luton

New name, new image

In cabaret at Watford

ending the day with a third performance somewhere else, day three would see us being driven to yet another base for a show, then straight to the airport to return home – pretty well exhausted usually, but the shows were always enjoyable and very worthwhile. We often appeared on makeshift stages, sometimes we would be in a cook house with dressing room in the kitchen, but this was during the troubles in Northern Ireland and the shows were always appreciated, although it was strange on occasion to see part of our audience suddenly pick up their rifles and file out because it was time for them to go on patrol.

We were always given a hospitable welcome in that we would be given a lovely big meal and drinks at each show, which meant on the second day in particular, we were all bursting with food and pretty well intoxicated by the time we went back to the hotel. We usually toured with a comedian and one of them said that by the third show on the second day, he would start getting confused as he was saying the same jokes he had already told twice that day and (probably due in some part to over imbibing), begin to wonder if he was repeating himself. In Belfast we also visited the hospital once where wounded British soldiers were being treated , going round the wards and having a chat with them. On one occasion a bedridden soldier we had spoken to, made a big kissing sound with his lips as Linda and I turned to go – Linda quipped "See your mouth's still working then!"

We were almost always collected at the airport and driven about by the same coach driver, who although he lived locally and had a strong Belfast accent, was originally a cockney. But on one tour, we had a substitute driver and on enquiring about our usual guy, were told that after he had dropped the last tour at the airport and was driving back to the depot, he stopped at traffic lights and a man starting banging on the coach door, when the driver opened it he was shot in the legs. After the man ran off, the driver managed to reach up and tear the fabric lining from the luggage rack and wrap it tightly around his knees, before driving himself to hospital. He took quite a while to recover, but far from being put off, as soon as he was able, he returned to duty driving the CSE shows for the British forces. Brave man.

When we did CSE shows we always stayed in hotels, but when we travelled around the U.K. performing in nightclubs we usually stayed in special guest houses for artistes and actors, known as "pro digs". These places had a different time schedule to normal guest houses in that breakfast was usually served between 11a.m and midday to allow artistes to lie in. The main meal was served around 5.30 pm to allow time for food to digest before their guests went on stage to sing, dance or act and most landladies would provide a little something to eat and drink left out for returning artistes - some sandwiches wrapped in foil, cake and biscuits and flasks of tea or coffee or a kettle to make your own. These places were also good for meeting other artistes, some performing in cabaret like ourselves, also actors, opera singers and bands and, on one occasion we spent a week with a magician and his partner - Clara the Clairvoyant Hen. Clara always joined us in the lounge, although she had her own spacious cage, as her owner never let her out of his sight. Clara had been trained to select playing cards and pick numbers etc. to appear as though she was mind reading and it would have taken a great deal of time and effort to find another suitable chicken and train it should anything ever happen to her, so she was totally cosseted and cared for.

Some digs were quite memorable. There was one in Nottingham run by a lady called Mrs Broomhead (Linda always referred to her as Mrs Brush head behind her back) who was a marvellous cook, but appeared to be in her eighties, wore a headscarf in the house and had terrible breathing difficulties. Her guests would all sit around one large table to eat and she would bring out the dinners two at a time and slowly walk around the table wheezing loudly as she put them in front of us. Rather reminiscent of Julie Walters' Two Soups sketch. We would all be looking at one another silently praying that she was not about to breath her last.

Some had pets, we often stayed with a couple in Birmingham who had no children but had turned their adorable west highland terrier Angus into a substitute. He was a real character and a champion at sitting up, cocking his head to one side and looking appealing, everyone fell for him. We also stayed once in Cardiff where the dog of the house Sandy was a handsome golden labrador cross, but his habits were less appealing. Every time he came into the lounge he would jump on the empty settee and start vigorously rogering the cushions for all he was worth. Bit of a distraction when ones trying to read or watch afternoon T.V.

Our favourite digs however were in Tuebrook, Liverpool run by a seemingly perfect landlady. The house was spotless and comfortable, the first one to have duvets on the beds instead of sheets and blankets. She was a lovely person, a good cook and always made us feel welcome. On one occasion we finished a show in St. Ives, Cornwall, having completed a week's cabaret, leaving there at midnight on Saturday and drove all night to Liverpool as, ironically, the club we were booked into was the only one in town to put on a lunchtime show on a Sunday! We went straight to the club and did the lunchtime show then went to Tuebrook. The landlady was horrified, gave us refreshments and told us to go to bed and she promised to wake us before dinner. A comedian we knew was always saying he was going to buy his agent a map - we knew just how he felt!

A highlight for us of 1974 was appearing for a week as the supporting act for Jack Jones at the Commodore Cabaret and Banqueting Suite in Nottingham, which was quite a prestigious venue at the time. That was a great week and we also met Susan George who was Jack's girlfriend at the time. That same year we spent a delightful two weeks in Malta where we found ourselves on the bill with an exciting dance troop with imaginative ideas and "seeds were sown" then which came to fruition some years later. The deal in Malta at that time was that acts worked without a fee but were given flights and full board at the hotel in return for three/four nightly cabaret shows over a fortnight. When we arrived at the hotel we were shown to pleasant rooms except for the fact they were inner rooms with no windows. We were straight down to the manager's office to complain. As Malta was the only country where the hotels didn't pay a fee to the cabaret acts we felt strongly that we should have proper quality holiday accommodation and we were moved into better rooms with sea views straight away. However a local agent also gave us a paid gig somewhere else on one of our nights off, so everything turned out well in the end, and we did end up with a profit and a holiday.

February 1975 was spent in Cairo, in cabaret at the Sheraton Hotel, we didn't stay in the hotel, but were given a house to live in along with a group of girl dancers who were also on the bill. The house was in such a state of disrepair and poor decoration that we all went to the hotel manager and complained. He promised to get everything fixed, but instead of moving us out, we had to put up with builders and decorators for the next two weeks. We all went out for much of the time as, apart from the mess, if Linda, myself or any of the dancers were in the house, the decorators would stand gawping and ogling us instead of working.

Of course we visited the Pyramids and also the museum in Cairo (three times, in fact) where we saw all the treasures of Tutankhamun without having to queue which was wonderful. One day the entire show and the band (who were Czechoslovakian) from the Sheraton were invited to a special day at the luxurious Mena House Hotel at Giza to celebrate the opening of their new swimming pool. A super day with fine food, beautiful sunshine, a lovely pool and great company.

Cairo was a noisy and chaotic place, and pretty filthy in some areas at that time, but never boring. Shopping was particularly interesting, Robin was trying shoes on one day, they were all hand made so varied in size and shape slightly, the assistant serving him kept going up to the floor above, leaning over the balcony and dropping shoes over until Robin found a left and right in the same style which both fit. Sadly though, many of the goods on sale in the shops were not well made. We bought some feather boas there which Linda and I decided to sew on to the hems of some costumes we were having made back home, the rich gold and brown feathers seemed a perfect match as the costumes were cream and gold with cutaway sides and very wide flared trousers.

When we arrived back in the U.K. we sewed on the feather boas and the first gig we had was in London. We sang and danced on the raised cabaret stage in the new costumes for the first part of the show and to our horror, the boas began to moult. By the end of the first four numbers the stage looked like a cock fight had taken place, there were gold and brown feathers everywhere. We had to laugh and joke about it with the audience, but it was not our finest moment.

In the spring of 1975 we were approached by an independent record producer who wanted to record us. After a search through material, we chose and recorded a song which we all liked and thought was commercial and the producer sent us off to London to a top show biz designer to have promotional outfits made - they were cherry red fitted suits with flared trousers with chequered lapels (it was the '70's) and we waited with baited breath for a release date. Then came the bombshell news that there was a dispute over who held the recording or publishing rights to this song and everything came to a standstill. The delay went on for weeks and in the end the producer decided to release another song we had recorded, written by a friend of ours who wrote under the name Gid Taylor. It was called Summer Song and was to be released on the Pye record label.

Prior to this we had been asked to do a summer season in Douglas, Isle of Man and I really didn't want to go as I was still haunted by memories of the fire at Summerland. We asked our agent to see what else he could come up with, but nothing else on offer at the time was as good as the season in Douglas, so in the end I gave in for the sake of my two colleagues.

We acquired a manager at this time called Bob James who was based at London Management and he gave us lots of work and one of the first gigs was supporting Frankie Vaughan on a bill that also included comedian Stu Francis and popular pianist Mrs Mills. We watched from the wings and observed Frankie Vaughan constantly encouraging his audience to sing along with all his songs and we had the distinct feeling that was partly because he couldn't remember most of the words.

In the months prior to the Douglas season starting, we toured the clubs around the UK and Linda and I took driving lessons with many different instructors in various towns, but we both took our tests on the same day in a town in the North East of England, where we had a favourite driving teacher who was thrilled (as were we) when we both passed on the same day. It meant we could then share the driving with Rob. We drove about in a big white Mercedes then because it had an enormous boot, perfect for carrying equipment and costumes.

When we went to the Isle of Man, however, Linda and I bought a small red car between us just to use for the three months we would be there, planning to sell it again at the end of the season. We appeared in the Kings club which was part of a complex on the seafront consisting of a theatre, nightclub and a casino. The immensely popular showband - The Grumbleweeds topped the bill at the theatre show which was compared by Dave Ismay, a comic who we worked with a lot, as he was also with London Management.

There were lots of artistes and musicians in Douglas for the summer and most of us became friends, so it was a very sociable season and I was glad I did go back in the end because it helped lay the ghosts to rest somehow. During the peak holiday weeks, various big name bands came and played Sunday concerts in the theatre for which we always had free seats, these included the Sweet, Status Quo, Marc Bolan, Hot Chocolate and the Rubettes. I remember the drummer from Status Quo taking us all out for a ride in his brand new Range Rover, one of the first off the assembly line.

Because of the aforementioned problems, the record we had made earlier in the year was not released until mid July which was somewhat late for its title "Summer Song", but it was played on the radio and Ed Stuart made it his "record of the Week", and we were performing it live to large audiences each night, only problem was no-one could buy it anywhere. Even in our home base of Margate, the record shops weren't stocking it – something was badly awry in the distribution department. It was so frustrating. We never got to the bottom of the problem and in the end the record producer just disappeared. .....who knows, if things had gone right we could have been famous......

Still, we really enjoyed that summer in the Isle of Man. One big mistake I made was agreeing to play in a ladies' charity football match one Saturday, our side was made up of singers, dancers and cocktail waitresses, the opposing side unexpectedly turned out to be a real ladies football team who totally trounced us. When we went on stage that night I had a lump the size of a conker on my right knee, which hurt like hell following a rough tackle in that game and I still get twinges in that knee.

During the season we all had the pleasure of attending the wedding of one of our fellow artistes at the Kings Club, singer Diane Chandler who married her manager Mike Bourne, the reception was held around a swimming pool at one of the hotels, it was a lovely day and a wedding during the season was definitely a 'first' for us.

We had rented a modern bungalow for the season and before it was over we held a big party for all the artistes, disc jockeys, musicians and dancers working in Douglas. It was a "shipwrecked" party and we decorated the bungalow with pictures and paper palm trees, we also saw some amazing costumes and outfits worn by the guests who had really entered into the spirit of the occasion. The following morning we found a pith helmet, a pair of hobnailed boots and an over sized bra (probably worn by one of the half dozen guys who had opted to come in drag) in the front garden and later a disc jockey from the local radio station told us that as he had been walking back into Douglas in the early hours of the morning, wearing shredded trousers (some other party guests thought he didn't look shipwrecked enough), he was stopped by a policeman who wanted to know why he was wandering the streets in this condition. "It's o.k. constable, I'm just returning home from a great showbiz party" he explained. The p.c. apparently said "Bloody hell, why don't I ever get invited to parties like that?" and let him go on his way.

Despite my fears it turned out to be a very good summer season after all.

We continued appearing in cabaret clubs around the UK and going on CSE shows for the forces. Most of these passed smoothly, but occasionally there would be an interesting 'blip' during the show. Usually incidents occurred during the song Bridge Over Troubled Water, in which we did a complete costume change. Linda and I would leave the stage to Rob who sang the first verse and chorus while we did a quick change backstage, then I would come back alone and sing the second verse and chorus while Rob changed, finally Linda and Rob would join me on stage for the final verse and chorus. It was very effective, most of the time. Once, we appeared at a very well known cabaret club in the Midlands and there was a large stag party seated around a table quite near the front of the stage. When it came to Bridge Over Troubled Water, Rob sang the first part and as I came back on stage and he went off to change, an argument broke out at the stag table, as I sang I observed the bouncers come over to try to keep the peace, but that didn't work and someone threw a chair at someone else, I carried on singing and by the time Rob and Linda came back on stage, their eyes wide, a full blown fight was in progress and no-one in the audience was watching us, every eye was on the scene before us which by now looked like something from an old John Wayne movie. We continued to sing this beautiful ballad, which sounded totally incongruous in the circumstances (apart from its title perhaps). Fortunately the bouncers managed to regain control and eject the troublemakers and surprisingly quickly everything returned to normal. We finished our spot in front of a now calm audience who had watched the rest of our show just as though nothing had happened.

In December 1975 we went to Israel to work in the Haifa Theatre Club for five weeks. We did encounter a bit of a hold up in the airport on our arrival in Israel as we had Egyptian stamps in our passports and for one awful moment we thought we would be not be allowed in the country. But after much discussion between themselves the officials involved decided we were harmless after all and let us in.

Haifa Theatre Club was a large and popular venue which put on a big show. There was an Israeli comic/compere, a young female Israeli singer, a striptease act and her husband (from Austria), a magician and his wife/assistant (from France) and we topped the bill. The only odd thing was that there was some sort of prohibition or license restriction at the time, so it always appeared that the audiences were drinking tea and coffee, when in fact they had booze which they brought in themselves served in cups – a bit like the American speakeasies of the 1920's.

We were given an apartment in Haifa just a short walk from the club, so we did a lot of our own cooking – although did buy some interesting items due to problems with language then, like the day we thought we'd bought sweet mince pies (it was December after all) and found later that we had added a custard sauce to savoury minced beef pies. As most of the Israeli citizens were relatively new arrivals from all over the globe, many of whom had not yet learned to speak Hebrew, there was confusion among all shoppers as people tried to communicate in bits and pieces of many languages, Yiddish and Russian being the most common.

There were a lot of stray cats in Haifa, that would often make us jump when they suddenly appeared out of the dustbins which had lightweight pop up lids. One particularly sweet one took to visiting us at the flat, she would tap with her paw on the kitchen window to attract our attention, she was really pretty and she was invited in sometimes.

Because of the lateness of the show – which began at midnight and the fact that we could not work on the Jewish Sabbath, we always had a very long weekend off. So we saw it as our chance to see as much as we could of Israel. When the show ended on Thursday we would go home, grab our bags and board a taxi to Jerusalem where we could link up with buses or a tour to somewhere else. We went to Jerusalem, Bethlehem, Capernaum, Hebron, Nazareth and the Sea of Galilee, where we ate the local speciality - St. Peter's fish. We usually travelled to Jerusalem by mini bus taxis, shared with other passengers and if there were any spare seats and we came across any Israeli soldiers, it was the custom to stop and give them a free lift.

We always walked to the club along a tree lined road, but on the walk back when it was dark, we had to be very quiet when we passed beneath one particular tree which was home to a huge colony of bats. There seemed to be hundreds of them residing in this one tree, I have no idea why. As long as we were quiet they stayed put, but if we were talking, the bats would start swooping down around our heads.

On Christmas eve we decided to go to Nazareth for a carol service. When we arrived we went first to the very amiable Abu Nazzer's Restaurant and had a dinner of Turkey legs with trimmings (almost Christmas dinner), before setting off on the walk up to the protestant church for the carol service. On the way up there we were jostled and spat at by the locals who were poor and apparently very much resented the huge and costly Roman Catholic Basilica that had been built there at the end of the same street. The mayor of Nazareth was a communist and saw the "wealthy" Christian westerners as intruders who were flaunting their money whilst the locals suffered deprivation. The new basilica, it seems, was to them a symbol of this Christian wealth in the midst of their poverty. So for us and our fellow churchgoers it was a really unpleasant "running of the gauntlet". On arrival at the much older protestant church we found it to be filled with a mix of all nationalities including many young people who were working on Kibbutz's. Once inside the crowded church we looked forward to singing carols, however before the service began, the minister had to make the unfortunate announcement that the organ had broken down and we would have to sing the carols unaccompanied – we would however be led in song by their resident choir. The choir sang well, the melodies familiar to all, but they sang in Arabic, the Dutch sang in Dutch, the Danish in Danish, the Brits in English and so on, making the words indistinguishable as all these languages came together in total incoherence, so that we all started together but gradually gave up the challenge leaving only the choir to battle on. Sadly, the carol service we had all looked forward to was a rather sad disappointment.

When we visited Jerusalem we saw the Mount of Olives, the Garden of Gethsemane, the Wailing Wall and the Dome of the Rock and also walked the path in the old city that Jesus took to Calgary, passing through the room where the last supper was supposed to have taken place. Standing on the spot where a mosaic star marks where the cross apparently stood was quite moving, until a Greek Orthodox priest kept saying "Psst, psst - buy a candle", over and over again until it became really annoying.

In Bethlehem, we visited the underground room which is believed to be the stable beneath the inn where Jesus was born, jointly cared for by three Christian churches from different countries. We also went to see the museum dedicated to the six million Jews who died at the hands of the Nazis in world war two and were told that the Israeli government had planted six million trees in their memory. When we alighted from the tour bus in Hebron however, we had to be escorted by armed Israeli soldiers as it was a troubled area and the Israeli feared Palestinian attacks there.

We enjoyed our work in Haifa and became good friends with the Austrian and French couples and so on Christmas Day invited them round to our flat for a bit of a get together. The magician and his wife brought champagne and chocolates with typical French finesse and though we didn't speak each others languages well, we all still managed to have a lovely day. The Austrian stripper complained about the poor quality of food items on sale in the market pronouncing indignantly "the chickens - they are not good looking!". It was policy in Israel at that time, as a relatively young growing country to export all their best produce and retain the less attractive second grade specimens for the home market.

We did go to a ballet gala while we were in Haifa featuring Valery and Galina Panov the great Russian dancers who had been imprisoned briefly in Russia after leaving the Kirov Ballet and applying to emigrate to Israel in 1972, they were eventually allowed to go to Israel in 1974, so we were very lucky to see them perform. We also went to the local cinema, which was not so enjoyable as the seats were wooden and the film wasn't exactly fun viewing either - Charlotte Rampling and Dirk Bogarde in The Night Porter about the sado-masochistic relationship between a young Jewess and her warder in a concentration camp. Between the seats and the subject matter, not the most comfortable outing!

On the last night of our stay at Haifa, we heard it was the stage hands' custom to play jokes. This night was no exception and the victim of the main joke was to be the poor striptease artiste or as she liked to be called "acrobatese" artiste as she and her husband had been acrobats for years, before finding that type of work work drying up.

She always began her act lying on a circular bed with satin and furs on it including a whole fox fur. On this night the guys had rigged up fine fishing line attached to the fox's head. Just as she rose from the bed so did the fox, appearing to suddenly stand on its hind legs. She screamed and the stage hands fell about. Must have given her quite a shock, though it did look funny.

In 1976, we spent a week at Caesar's Palace, Luton with comic Mike Reid and one night I was asked to help Mike present a local pool's winner with a cheque for £12,000, which doesn't seem a lot now, but it was worth more in the '70's. I wasn't too thrilled at having to don a sash with Vernon's Pools splashed across it for the presentation though.

Apart from the U.K. clubs and theatres, as Trilogy we had many interesting jobs overseas. We spent a month in Lagos, Nigeria, which was probably the scariest place we visited. On our arrival it took about two hours just to get out of the airport, with all the red tape, which could be overcome with bribes apparently, but we just had to put up with it. On our way into the city, we saw a body being lifted out of the water, not an uncommon occurrence according to our driver, in fact when we went shopping there was also a dead body lying on the pavement, covered with newspaper, which no-one had claimed, so it just stayed there for a few days.

The Federal Palace hotel turned out to be very pleasant though, set amid lovely gardens and we were given an air conditioned bungalow in the grounds and were told we would eat our meals in the hotel executive's section of the dining room. Unfortunately when we went to rehearse with the house band who were from Spain, it transpired they were unable to read music. It took about fourteen hours' rehearsal over three days to get them to "learn" just forty minutes worth of our songs, so our first show was rather short. We were on the bill with another English act, Chantelle – three girl dancers who worked to backing tapes, so had no problem with the band. That was the moment when we finally decided that even though the sound of a good live band accompanying the act was best, taped backing would be the future way to go. The band worked hard however and did their best to learn our other songs, so that we could perform as well as we could for the rest of our stay.

We liked to go down to the beach and buy fruit from the wandering fruit sellers there and also enjoyed shopping for local arts and crafts, but we soon learned not to shop for souvenirs when cruise ships docked at Lagos as the local artisans all put their prices up on those days and refused to barter with us.

We made a few good friends there and generally had fun, but things could get irritating, many of the hotel staff were incompetent as they were not selected on experience and capability, but on which tribe they belonged to, and I don't believe any of us ever got the drinks we had actually ordered, always a surprise - but when the water went off at the hotel for an entire weekend that was the last straw and we were therefore really thankful to one ex pat friend, Rex, who lived in a large house and had his drivers pick up both acts and take us all back to his home where he kindly put us all up until the water came back on again.

Rex had built up a successful business in Nigeria, but at the time of the military coup he was ordered to hand his business over to a local chief, as were all western business owners, and he was kept on as Managing Director on a salary. Fortunately for him, he got along with his Chief, which he told us, was not the case for many other business owners.

During our stay, the Nigerian government decided to install traffic lights in the city for the first time. Despite some publicity leading up to the big "switch on", chaos ensued as there were still many drivers who didn't know what they were and why they should stop. It was soon decided to switch them off again until the people could be educated further in the interest of public safety.

One day we were taken for a day out which involved crossing a large murky looking creek in boats that were very flat, like punts, and seemed a bit too close to the filthy brown water for my liking, which apparently had crocodiles residing in it, making for a rather nervous crossing. Fortunately we survived the outing and had no close encounters of the "croc" kind.

When we flew out of Lagos at the end of our month I must admit to heaving a big sigh of relief that we were still in good health, free from malaria and had not been involved a road accident (apparently at that time the passenger in a taxi was considered liable in any accident as they had employed the driver).

At sometime during this period, Linda and I changed our names to Linda Christensen (her mother's maiden name) and Carole St. James (for no particular reason other than I liked the sound of it) and we stuck with these.

On 5th December 1976 we appeared at a major charity concert at the Victoria Palace in London for the National Society for Mentally Handicapped Children, it was a huge show headlined by Roy Castle. Freddie and the Dreamers and Bernie Clifton were also on the bill and the event was organised by Jimmy Saville, or at least his "people" although he did not attend. However, we were asked to appear again the following year in December 1977 with Kenny Ball and his Jazzmen and Keith Harris and Orville (Keith Harris wasn't happy I recall because he had been told the Society's Patron H.R.H. The Queen Mother would be in attendance and she wasn't). The now horrifyingly disgraced Jimmy Saville was there on that occasion, but I have no recollection of meeting him I am pleased to say.

In January 1977, we had an interesting trip for C.S.E out to Salalah, Oman and the island of Masirah to entertain the RAF who would soon be leaving and handing over their airbase over to the Sultan of Oman for his air force. We went out there with Chantelle - the same girl dance group we had worked with in Nigeria, comedian Jimmy Marshall and Terry Lightfoot's Jazz band. As we approached the airstrip in Salalah, I was invited into the cockpit and asked to give our position to the controller on the other end of the radio, on the grounds that he and his colleagues hadn't heard a female voice in a few months. He was pleasantly shocked and the pilot and crew thought it hilarious.

However the flight between Salalah and Masirah was not so comfortable as we were taken by a Hercules (normally used for transporting military vehicles), where the only place to sit is around the sides of the aircraft and the only toilet is in a contraption suspended in the air which has to be lowered should anyone require it. Fortunately no-one did, though we all felt a bit queasy as the Hercules flew at a much lower altitude than a normal plane.

Apart from that it was a really enjoyable trip, the shows went well and we were entertained too. Among the treats we experienced were being taken up in a Wasp helicopter and given a great view of the area and surrounding sea which was crystal clear; being invited guests at an "Arabian Nights" Fancy dress party in the Officers mess where we dined on shark vindaloo and barracuda; going "Bondu bashing" - searching for fossils in the rocks of the desert and being given a ride on what the RAF chose to call "the Masirah State Railway" but was in reality more like Thomas the Tank Engine.

The journey back home turned out to be rather interesting too as the RAF were due to fly us back to Brize Norton via Cyprus to collect school children of servicemen there who were going back to school in England, which was fine, until they were also ordered by the British Labour government to make a detour to Nairobi, Kenya in order to pick up a government minister and his entourage. The RAF officer who broke this news to us was positively apoplectic with rage about this as the RAF had to pay £2,000 for landing rights at Nairobi and put all the passengers up in a hotel for the night. The artistes on the show were annoyed because we were all going to be a day late back from the trip, which was really inconvenient for most people, particularly those with other gigs to get to and, of course all the school children were going to be late back which was worrying for their schools and their parents. There were of course plenty of civilian airlines flying out of Nairobi to London which they could have used. Just to add insult to injury, the following day, we all boarded the aircraft and then sat there for a whole hour while a "first class private section" was installed to accommodate this minister and his cronies.

We went on more CSE shows to Northern Ireland and also experienced a very windy trip to the Outer Hebrides. The landing of our flight there was pretty unnerving – as the cross winds were wild and aircraft were not always able to land. It so happened, we were cheerfully informed by a member of the crew, that we were being flown that day by a pilot known as "Mad Mike". Can't say this information instilled much confidence, however he made it. It seems his method was to come in low and suddenly drop on to the landing strip with a bang, jolting us all almost out of our seats.

The high winds kept up during our first show and we had been allotted a caravan to use as a dressing room, parked adjacent to the back door leading to the stage. Poor Linda was first to open the caravan door to cross into the building and as the door opened, a gust of wind took it and Linda literally flew out of the caravan hanging onto the door handle. Fortunately, though shaken, she was not injured. The show went down very well though.

Whilst there we were taken out to a bar which was a typical Crofter's cottage, but inside one entire wall was covered in shelves containing hundreds of different whiskeys - no other drinks were available. We also visited a silversmith who worked from another croft. Most of the RAF stationed there spent their time fly fishing and drinking fine whisky. On the whole, we had a very pleasant stay there and I still remember the dog belonging to one of the officers, a beautiful, crazy red setter who went by the glorious name of Seamus O'Hooligan!

Fortunately weather conditions had calmed down sufficiently on the day we were due to leave again, so the plane was able to take off and return us home without any delay.

April 1977 was a particularly good month for Trilogy. We had another trip for CSE this time to Gibraltar with comic Dave Butler and a crazy conjurer known as the "Incredible Christopher". The weather was fabulous and it was really interesting to go into the caves, some of which were closed to the public and only used by the Ministry of Defence and of course, back above ground to be entertained/harassed by the apes.

But the biggest highlight of that month for us was being booked as a support act to the great Morecambe and Wise for a weekend at the Bristol Hippodrome (two matinees and two evening shows). We watched every one of their performances from the wings. They were the most professional act I've ever seen. They were also lovely people. Between shows Eric invited us to sit in his dressing room and chat – as he said Ernie would always entertain all the backstage v.i.p visitors in his dressing room, which Eric said was more Ernie's "cup of tea", whereas Eric preferred to be quieter.

That year we also worked with Larry Grayson, Marti Caine, Dick Emery, Roy Hudd, Little and Large and several times with Jimmy Tarbuck and Kenny Lynch

During the Trilogy years, Robin had sold his café and taken the lease on an empty shop in the High street in Margate and I decided to go into partnership with him and we transformed it into a "western style" coffee shop/restaurant called El Ranchero, we introduced real beef burgers and pizzas to Margate, but it took a while to get established as people were slow to try new things in Margate in those days. However, with Robin's older sister managing the cafe and us working there when we weren't away singing, it became popular. Upstairs we had lots of rooms in the building, so were able to let some out during the summer season to artistes appearing at the Winter Gardens Theatre, it worked well. So well in fact that we decided to open another coffee shop in Herne Bay in partnership with a friend. We opened that in a fanfare of glory, adding a greetings card and gift shop in the upstairs area and at Christmas, we had a Santa Claus. My dad came down from Manchester to play the part and very well too, one small boy saying "he was the best Santa" he had seen.

That summer we decided to accept a summer season touring Pontins' Holiday Camps along the south coast so we would be back at home on Saturday and Sunday each week, giving us a chance to keep an eye on the business and also freeing us to do some other one night stands and Sunday concerts.

Although the tour was well paid, we didn't really find it enjoyable. On three nights we would perform at two holiday camps per night at which there would be a resident "Bluecoat Show". The snag was that the Bluecoats would always perform their show at the prime time and we and other artistes on the circuit touring Pontin's holiday camps would find ourselves stuck with the unpopular slots, either too early when children were being taken to bed and adults were buying their bingo tickets, or late when people were either a bit drunk or, in the early and late part of the season, when the audiences were mostly senior citizens, getting ready to go to bed and standing up mid performance to go and queue for their cocoa. The other acts on the circuit all moaned about it and one comedian, lost it one evening halfway through his act and gave the pensioners leaving their seats a real telling off! Occasionally in the mid season though, we would also perform at Sunday concerts with stars of the time in seaside theatres which was enjoyable.

We had by then changed the Mercedes for a Ford Zodiac car, which also had a huge boot that could take our equipment and costumes, and we took turns with the driving. One day, when it was my turn and I was in the fast lane of the motorway approaching London, the engine suddenly cut out and I had the terrifying experience of steering a car without power which was slowing down of its own accord across three lanes of traffic to the hard shoulder. We made it safely thank goodness, the only injury being to our bank balance as a new engine was needed and was not cheap. It seems the car had run out of oil, but the warning light had not come on.

Apart from one or two highlights, like the weekend at Bristol with Morecambe and Wise, I felt that was a summer season best forgotten. We had always taken lots of photographs in summer, but I don't seem to have taken any during that season and we were all glad when it was over.

That car must have been fated, as another time it was stolen from an airport hotel car park and when we eventually got it back it had been pretty vandalised inside, there were cigarette burns on the dashboard and it was filthy. When we cleaned it up we found a set of thieves keys under one of the seats which I tried to hand in to the Margate police, but they wouldn't take them and told me to keep them! Didn't want the paperwork obviously.

In late December 1977, we had another great trip to the United Arab Emirates. We worked about nine days with Jimmy Edwards and then three days with Ronnie Corbett making a very memorable Christmas and New Year for us. During the time spent with Jimmy Edwards, I think I laughed more than at any other time in my life. He was such fun, we were literally crying with laughter at times.

We stayed in a bungalow with our own chef for the first three days, which was on the ex pat workers' base of a company called Dutco Pauling in Dubai where we performed our first show. Jimmy who was also staying in another bungalow with his "road manager" - an effete young man called Raymond, played Christmas Carols on his euphonium for everyone on a very sunny Christmas eve morning and we all sang. At some point during the tour, Jimmy lost patience with Raymond, who never actually lifted a finger to help Jimmy with his instruments and props, and promptly sent him packing back to England. Raymond later got his slimy revenge by "outing" Jimmy to the Sunday papers though.

Whilst in the Emirates we also worked at the Hilton Hotels in Abu Dhabi and Bahrain. There was an outdoor pool at the Abu Dhabi Hilton with some guest rooms surrounding the pool. Late one evening I was walking past said pool on my way back to my room and Jimmy was returning to his when he turned to me and said "I don't think I'll go to bed yet, think I'll just sit here for a while….. and play my hunting horn". I just burst out laughing, the thought of the hotel guests sleeping in the poolside rooms being woken by the sound of a hunting horn being played by an eccentric Englishman in the middle of the night was too much.

We were also booked in at the Gulf Hotel in Doha but almost didn't make it. It seems the agent had made an error with our visas arranging just a single entry visa for Doha, but we had already done one show there. As we arrived at the airport and showed our passports, an official stopped us and the next moment we were being escorted by soldiers with guns back into the airport departure lounge to be put on the next plane out of there, fortunately that flight turned out to be going to Bahrain where the agent lived. The agent then had to contact a Sheikh – interrupting his dinner, we heard, - who was in a position to sanction our visit to Doha, thankfully strings were pulled and we returned a day later than planned. That should have been our day off which we expected to enjoy around the pool at the hotel, instead we were going backwards and forwards and not knowing whether we would be sent home, at least we weren't shot or thrown in jail!

Despite the difficulties with drinking alcohol in that part of the world, Jimmy Edwards always managed to get hold of champagne, once cracking open a case that had been won in a raffle by someone, as the unfortunate ticket holder was away at the time. Jimmy could drink the clock round and somehow reach a point when he would appear totally sober again.

At one of the airports, an elderly Arab gentleman spotted Linda and very excitedly began to fire questions in Arabic at Jimmy, who had to ask an airport official to interpret what he was saying, the official said the old man thought Linda was beautiful and would like to offer Jimmy many camels for her. Jimmy shouted something about the cattle on his farm wouldn't really get along with camels, but then took out his cigar cutter and held it up to the old man's nose, saying "Do you know what this is?" whilst operating the snipping mechanism and shooing him away. He then told the airport workers to stand up straight and take their hands out of their pockets before marching us all off.

One evening we were sitting at the bar in the Hilton in Bahrain and Jimmy was making us laugh as usual, when two young men sitting next to me asked who he was. I explained that he was a famous comedian in the UK and they said they were German and would love to meet him. When I told Jimmy (who had flown spitfires during the war) that these German gentlemen would like to meet him he looked at them and in a very loud voice bellowed "Germans! Germans! I spent nigh on six years trying to kill you bastards!" Fortunately they thought this was hysterical and an international incident was averted. Another time we were in a hotel where we were due to entertain a huge party of oil workers and their wives who had gathered in their finery in the bar adjacent to the function room where we were to perform. Unfortunately the hotel were providing the sound system speakers and the people employed to set them up could not get them working. This was causing a huge hold up, we couldn't do a sound check, the audience could not be admitted and were becoming restless and probably increasingly inebriated in the bar, meanwhile in the function room tensions were reaching boiling point.

Suddenly Jimmy said "Well I think I will go to my room, get into my tuxedo, then I'm going to stand in the middle of the audience in the bar and shout "F**k" at the top of my voice!" We all cracked up, he certainly broke the tension and shortly after that the sound system speakers sprang to life and we were thankfully able to get on with the show.

He could also be very kind, on Christmas Day we three found ourselves setting up equipment, doing sound checks and rehearsing while everyone else was enjoying a Christmas dinner, but Jimmy made sure that three dinners were kept aside for us. When he heard that we were going to be working with Ronnie Corbett the following week, he confided in me that he had once upset Ronnie and felt really ashamed and sorry about it. I got the impression that he wanted me to pass that on to him. We were very sad to leave Jimmy at the end of this tour and he said it was the most fun he had ever had on a trip. (Tragically we never saw him again as he passed away the following year, probably his liver, but I can't help feeling that Raymond's vindictive dealings with the press may have hastened his decline).

However, we then met up with Ronnie Corbett who was also great company. We had three gigs together, and were all staying at the Bahrain Hilton. The first two gigs were in The British Club. Robin set up our pa system for Ronnie to use for which he was really grateful and he went over a storm with the Brits, he was very funny. But our final night was New Year's Eve at the Hilton. Not a favourite gig date for most acts as audiences tend to be loud and drunk. Not so bad for us however, being a visual musical act and appearing early in the evening, though people were already getting a bit silly and throwing all the usual novelties and poppers around during our performance, but our hearts went out to Ronnie Corbett as he walked out to face a multi national audience, many of whom did not speak English well enough to understand jokes when sober and were by then, very drunk indeed. It was a rather humiliating experience for a great performer and in retrospect, a huge misbooking by the agent, but he battled through it and even managed to have fun afterwards joining in the dancing with us and doing a memorable highland fling. I decided I should pass on to him what Jimmy had said about being really sorry that he had once upset him and I think he was surprised, but also pleased.

In April 1978 we worked in a club in the very attractive town of Stavanger in Norway with its distinctive white clapper board houses, which we really enjoyed, being our first time in Scandinavia, and that was followed by a tour of British military bases in Northern Germany for CSE. The region we were working in was known for its hunting and shooting and so we found wild boar and other game on the menu at the hotel.

They also served goose fat as a starter, which was definitely one to miss as I found out to my dismay having mistakenly ordered it from the German menu.

Changes were in the air that year as Robin and I decided to sell the Herne Bay coffee shop after our partner unexpectedly pulled out, finding it had become a bit of a millstone and decided to concentrate on our show business life instead. We also changed the name of the act to Stephen Gold with Flame, Robin using his second name of Stephen and adding Gold. So from here on he is referred to as Stephen.

On December 3rd 1977 we once more took part for the third year running in the Startime charity concert for the National Society for Mentally Handicapped Children, this time at the Old Vic theatre. The Old Vic's stage has a steep rake which is difficult enough to dance on, but proved to be a serious problem for Basil Brush or rather his puppeteer Howard Williams, who had to operate Basil from inside a large box on wheels. Under normal circumstances, Basil Brush would appear two or three times throughout the show for short periods, due to the cramped conditions his other self was obliged to work in, but because of the rake the wheeled box just wanted to roll off the stage during rehearsals. Poor Howard had to rethink his whole performance resulting in him enduring one long spot in the second half in acute discomfort crouched for a long time in the box which had to be nailed down.

Chapter 8
STEPHEN GOLD WITH FLAME

In the summer of 1978 we were booked by dynamic theatre producer, Dick Condon for his new summer show in Cromer, Norfolk. Having totally revived the fortunes of the Theatre Royal in Norwich, Dick Condon had been asked to do the same for the Pier Pavilion Theatre in Cromer, Norfolk with a summer season. We weren't too keen at first as there was talk of a possible season with a really big name then – Des O'Connor, but as time went on and no confirmation seemed forthcoming for the Des O'Connor show and Dick Condon was really keen on booking us, we decided to sign up for Cromer. Topping the bill were Millican and Nesbitt, the close harmony act who had won several times on Opportunity Knocks and Scottish Music hall star Denny Willis, along with comedian Billy Crockett, conjurer Ian Simpson, ourselves and the Pat Adams dancers. Right up to the last minute we really weren't sure whether this booking was going to be modern enough for us.

However the season turned out to be a huge success, with the show having to be extended for an extra week and was to be the most enjoyable summer season we ever did.

We were a happy cast and instead of just performing our own acts, we all became involved in production pieces and helping each other, except for Millican and Nesbitt who just came on and sang at the end. This arrangement made the time pass quickly and was also more enjoyable for us and the audiences. We rented a house for the summer from a delightful couple in Cromer, Don and Vera Bartman, who we also became good friends with and they had a boat on the Norfolk Broads which they would sometimes invite us on for a Sunday cruise and lunch on board.

During the season, a BBC T.V. production team turned up in Cromer to film some sketches for Spike Milligan's Q8 show and were keen to use Equity members who were performing on the North Norfolk Coast as extras for some of his sketches.

Spike Milligan and the BBC cast and crew stayed at the interestingly named Hotel de Paris in Cromer which had a tower room that at the time was used as a store for spare mattresses etc. However Spike Milligan decided he wanted to sleep in the tower and the shows director, Ray Butt who had worked with Spike a long time, persuaded the management to let him sleep there as it would make life easier for everyone. We heard that he apparently put his bedding into the bath and slept in that.

A small group from our show spent a day filming for Q8 on a duck farm in the Norfolk countryside. Linda, choreographer Pam and I had to be dressed in nun's habits for the first sketch. We were transformed into nuns as soon as we arrived at the farm, but when asking directions to the ladies loos, were informed the unit had not brought any, but we could walk down the road to a nearby pub and use theirs. So a trio of nuns walked along this country road until we came across the pub. We entered by a side door where a young man was cleaning glasses behind the bar. At sight of us his jaw dropped and he walked out sideways from the bar still polishing a glass, without a word and never taking his eyes off us. In his place a woman appeared asking politely if she could help us. I suppose we should have explained that we were recording a T.V. show and not real nuns, but the moment was too delicious. I smiled benignly and asked in my sweetest tone whether we could use the ladies toilets. "Of course you may" replied the woman reverently. "Thank you my dear" said I and we walked with dignity into the ladies room where we promptly collapsed with laughter. "Good thing she didn't notice your red nail polish Pam". When we returned to the farm we were told what was required of us. We were to sit on a steamroller and sing "All things Bright and Beautiful" whilst it rolled over the Archbishop of Canterbury who was staked out on the path, in order to rid him of his "sinful urges"

- typical Spike Milligan humour. The steamroller was extremely hot and the crew had to put cardboard between our backs and the engine to protect us from the heat. During and in between his other sketches Spike had us all in fits of laughter as he was even funnier off set than he was on. We and his regular cast and crew were laughing all day, it was a miracle they got any takes at all..

Another filming day was spent on a quiet beach whilst people wearing traffic warden uniforms and Hitler moustaches ran about with parking meters representing bazookas, firing and shouting in German in some mock up of the Normandy landings. Unfortunately, there was a family on the beach that day who hurriedly packed up their belongings and departed for their car in much haste. The car had a German number plate.

Later that evening, the cast and some crew members from the film unit came to watch our show and had taken seats across the whole of the front row. There was a point in the show where we all dressed as cockney costers and would stroll from one side of the stage to the other, singing "Underneath the Arches". The line would start with three of us, then as we reached the wings and turned, two more people would join the line and we would walk and sing in time to the music to the other side and be joined by two more and so on. This night, on the very last turn as the full line up crossed the stage singing we were met by the sight of the entire front row sporting Hitler moustaches. Most of us were desperately trying not to "corpse" without much success and the rest of the audience had no idea why.

After having so much fun that week we decided to invite all the cast and crew to a "Cheese and Wine" party at our house. (Cheese being a cheap option in those days), but when they turned up they also brought along the production's caterers and as I held open the front door, tray upon tray of party food goodies were brought in. What a great end to the week.

We also had an invitation to attend a special reception at Anglia Television to honour Eric Morecambe and present him with a portrait. Having thoroughly enjoyed appearing with Morecambe and Wise at Bristol, we happily accepted and spent a very nice couple of hours at the studios along with other artistes appearing on the Norfolk coast that summer, including Lenny Henry, Larry Grayson, Frank Carson and Bobby Knutt who I would later find myself working with in the Falklands.

Of course, having made so many good friends we had to finish the season with another Shipwrecked/Castaways party, which was great fun and the sight of our female stage manager dressed (and blacked) up as Man Friday was something wondrous to behold. It was a truly memorable season. The pier at Cromer has continued to have a summer variety show every year since that first one.

Lesley Crowther was another great entertainer who we spent a week in cabaret with in Norfolk. We all stayed in the same hotel which was fortunate for Lesley as one night he had so many fans buying him drinks that we could see he was getting extremely drunk and so decided we would hang around and give him a lift back to the hotel, which he gratefully accepted. We practically had to carry him into the hotel, which wasn't easy as he was a very tall man. He was good company though and we met him again when he came down to Margate for a Sunday Concert at the Winter Gardens and after rehearsal he came back to our place for something to eat before the show.

I remember him telling us a story about his days hosting the children's T.V. show Crackerjack. Being a live show for children it was of course imperative that nobody swore, so it became his habit on the final sound check before the audience was admitted, to come out with a quick fire tirade of expletives into the microphone to get it out of his system so to speak. One day a group of brownies were being shown around the set and were all in the director's box along with their leader when the final sound check had to be done and no-one had thought to tell Lesley that they were there, so the tirade of swear words poured out of the speakers as usual. He didn't tell us whether the shocked group stayed for the show, but I suspect they never saw Leslie Crowther in quite the same light again.

In January 1979 we were booked to appear as the headline act at the Casino in Estoril, Portugal, a glamorous venue with a casino and two entertainment rooms within the same building, the main cabaret room had a large stage which incorporated a circular hydraulic section which rose up from the basement and a catwalk into the auditorium, along with fabulous lighting. The lavish show consisted of a glamorous floorshow, a speciality act, a Portuguese act and a headline act. That month we were the top of the bill, the speciality act was a wonderful 82 year old Chinese diablo aficionado called Wong Mow Ting, a Portuguese singer - Helen Torres and a spectacular dance show from the USA - Finnan's Follies. The second room was an intimate late night cabaret room which featured just one 'exotic' act. When we were there, it was Angele and Mara, two Spanish girls who were also a "couple". They were really pleasant girls, Angele was a trained ballet dancer, and their dream was to open a sausage shop together in Spain one day, so they travelled worldwide performing their erotic dance act which was in fact, very balletic, but they would not work in their own country Spain as, in their words, they would be expected to be "too pornographica" there.

We really enjoyed the month at Estoril, we got on really well with all our fellow artistes and dancers and the show was well attended and we had a surprise too.

One day the manager called us in to say the casino would be hosting a special fund raising event featuring various Portuguese children's choirs and dance groups in the main show room and it was to be in the presence of various members of floating European royalty and nobility, including we were told by the manager, a Duchess of Bulgaria, the Arch Duke of Austria, Maria of Spain and a Prince of Portugal and headed by Her Royal Highness Princess Grace of Monaco who was Patron of the charity involved, and he would like us to appear and sing a couple of songs as well. So we had an unexpected and delightful extra show and performed in front of the cool and sophisticated Princess Grace.

A couple of months later in March 1979, we went out to Singapore to appear for a month at the Hotel Shangri-la, a fabulous trip, but not everything went to plan. The flight took eighteen hours and we arrived in Singapore in a heatwave, only to find that two of our suitcases had not arrived with us. Linda's and mine, it turned out, had gone on to Australia. So we found ourselves having to wear the same clothes we had travelled in for another twenty four hours, as we obviously couldn't borrow any stuff from Stephen and it was a Sunday when the shops were closed.

The hotel though was fabulous, each night at midnight the carpets were changed in the lifts to say "Have a nice Monday" "Tuesday" etc. and Linda and I had a gorgeous room with view of the swimming pool and gardens. Fortunately we were not due to perform for a couple more days and at lunchtime on the day we were to make our debut, with press in attendance, we went into the coffee shop to have a light lunch. Stephen ordered a Reuben sandwich, Linda and I had something different. We then went to do some last minute rehearsals, but Stephen began to feel unwell and eventually had to make a dash for the nearest loo. By the evening he was so stricken with food poisoning, he was dehydrating fast and his bed was surrounded by the hotel's doctor and at least three hotel executives who were very worried indeed, partly because they would have to tell the press and public that there would be no grand opening show that night, but were also aware that it may have been caused by something served in their restaurant. Some of them looked more green than Stephen. He was taken to hospital by ambulance (which we had to pay £10 up front for) and kept in overnight and put on a drip. It was an interesting ward as there were no glass windows and birds could and did fly in and out among the patients However the doctors had him back on his feet the next day and the opening night was rearranged for the following night after his return to the hotel. Happily there were no more hitches and we actually had a really enjoyable stay at the Shangri la. We appeared in the cabaret room on the top floor, there was also a disco and another great bar built like a ship in the basement where a very good Chinese country and western band had a residency. Singapore was beautiful and we visited various attractions, including the wonderful orchid nurseries, the botanic gardens, the famous Raffles hotel, the Chinese gardens, Jurong bird park, Sentosa Island (via cable car) and spent a very interesting evening in Bugis street, where at the stroke of midnight the glamorous lady boys paraded up and down looking beautiful, you could have your fortune told by the palm readers, various vendors came round selling goods and delicious food was served from street stalls. We got in that night at around 4.30 a.m..

While we were in Singapore we also met up with my cousin Beryl and her husband Eric who was a pilot for BOAC and frequently had stopovers there and we spent a lovely morning with them sitting outside in the garden cafe of the Mandarin Hotel. The shops there were fantastic and Linda and I had a great time buying clothes, as they were all smaller sizes and shoes over size 5 were almost impossible to find. Sometimes it pays to be petite!

One afternoon we performed on a television show, where we mimed to our record "Summer Song" which went very well. We were however asked to sew up part of our costumes so as not to show too much cleavage!

What had started out rather badly actually turned out to be a really wonderful trip, though it finished as it began, with a bit of a disaster – for me anyway. In the earlier part of the evening before our last show we were taken for farewell drinks at another hotel in the town with a group of people. I accepted a lift back in the sports car of one of the hotel executives, not realising he'd drunk more than he should and as he turned the last corner before reaching the hotel, he misjudged it and hit the rather high kerb, bursting the front tyre in the process and I shot up in the air and down again with a bump (there were no seat belts in the car) banging my right elbow on the divider between the seats and jarring my shoulder. I didn't want to go to the hospital, I just wanted to get in the hotel and get ready for our last performance. The last show was great and Linda and I were presented with bouquets of red roses and Steve with a beautiful lei garland from the grateful club management. Super evening, but next morning at breakfast I couldn't lift my right arm up to drink my coffee. As we were about to fly home I decided I would wait until we arrived back in the U.K. before going to see a doctor. It turned out I didn't need any surgery fortunately, but because I hadn't been treated straight away I now had a weakness that would stay with me, stiff necks were a recurring problem for years, until one day when I went to see a clairvoyant who gave me healing and to my astonishment the pain left me immediately and have never had a stiff neck since. I still have some weakness in my right upper arm though, which I always feel when doing yoga stretches.

In 1979 more changes were in the air, as Linda had fallen in love with Graeme, the owner of the recording studio where we used to record our backing tracks and she decided to leave the act and move in with him, marrying him the following year. Stephen and I sold the Margate coffee shop and bought a three story house in Westbrook, Margate for a good price as it had a sitting tenant on the middle floor, but as she was a very old lady who was in hospital at the time, we thought it worth the risk. This fortunately turned out to be the case as our absent tenant never returned to her flat having been told she should go into a nursing home and so gave up the tenancy. We were then able to create a really useful layout with a top floor flat which we could rent out, three bedrooms on the middle floor and a music room, office and kitchen/diner on the ground floor.

After much thought, Stephen and I decided to advertise for a replacement for Linda and to keep the act going. We held auditions and took on a girl called Sandy. We rehearsed, had new photos taken and began working in the clubs again. Things went fairly well but we noticed that every now and again, Sandy would have a day when she would go very quiet and moody for no apparent reason and on one occasion in her home town, she left the room to ask a chef in the venue we were working (whom she knew) if there was any chance of a sandwich or snack. Stephen and I waited for ages but we never saw her again that evening – it transpired she had a big row with the chef and had stormed off. Looking back I suppose it could have been severe PMT, but though we found her behaviour odd we didn't foresee what was to come.

We were approached by an agent from Amsterdam to take a contract to appear in a nightclub there. Stephen and I were a bit hesitant as we knew that nightclubs in Europe could be real dens of iniquity and often female artistes were expected to double as club hostesses, so we discussed this with the agent and agreed that it would written into our contract that we would not be expected to mix with the customers.

The agent seemed a decent guy and the contract had been signed by the club owner, stating that we would not be expected to sit in the club. However on our arrival we found that the club was open until 4 a.m. and we were expected to appear in three short spots between midnight and 3 a.m. Then we were shown our dressing room – this turned out to have a ceiling height of 4.5 ft. Maximum, making it impossible to fully stand up and therefore, in the periods between shows, it would have been too uncomfortable to remain in there. So we decided we would sit in the club, but only in a well lit corner near the doorway and keep ourselves to ourselves. The next day the agent called us into his office and said that the owner of the club had complained that we had not sat in the main club and mixed with people! We refused, the club management were not going to back down, so the agent ended up pulling us out of there and sending us to another venue which he said had very good stage facilities and where we would definitely not have to mix with the clientèle, what's more we only had to perform one show per night – perfect.

When we arrived we found wonderful dressing rooms in the basement with showers and comfortable armchairs, impressed, we asked directions to the stage and were told to go up the stairs, but we went up two flights by mistake and came out on a floor which looked like a hotel as there were beautifully appointed bedrooms, the doors of each were open wide as they were not occupied. Realising our mistake we went back down one floor where we found the entrance to the stage which had proper stage lighting and a set of heavy curtains fronting on to the club room. We were really pleased and that night when we arrived at the venue, we found several attractive girls, who we presumed to be the club's hostesses relaxing in the large lounge-like dressing room. When it was cabaret time we went up the stairs, on stage and waited for our taped backing music to begin and curtains to open. As they opened we stepped forward to sing and all three of us struggled not to burst out laughing as the penny finally dropped on sight of our surroundings - scarlet flocked wallpaper, rosy lighting, sofas occupied by business suited men with beautiful girls draped all over them around the room and erotic Victorian oil paintings on the walls, that we were in a brothel – albeit a high class one.

This was a first, but we sang and danced and the audience loved us, they all clapped along and cheered like mad at the end of our performance. It couldn't have gone better.

However, the next day we were summoned once more to see the agent who apologised and said he had been asked to withdraw us from this venue. We protested that we had gone down an absolute storm with the audience and left them wanting more… "That is precisely why I can't send you back there" he said. Apparently we had been too distracting and so the real business of getting men to buy overpriced drinks then take a girl up to one of the bedrooms had taken a back seat. We were replaced by a conjurer.

The agent was genuinely sorry we could tell, and he did manage to get us a one night stand in Rotterdam, but we felt it was time to take matters into our own hands. When in Rotterdam, we found another agent who dealt with discotheques and musical acts who appeal to the young people of Holland, so rather than risk any more dubious nightclubs we did some gigs for him which were great. The discos were all fabulous, beautifully decorated venues and we went down well, being a pop based act. We only worked in a few as the bookings were too last minute, the agent saying he could have given us lots more if he had known about us a couple of months previously. So it was a strange trip, but not a total disaster, in fact we enjoyed all the work apart from the first club.

In November 1979, we went on a tour of venues in Norway, both north and south, which turned out to be very eventful. Most of these shows went really well, but one night in Stavangar, in the large cabaret/disco room of the hotel, we had a very drunk and noisy table to our right. These awful people managed to completely ruin our show by shouting out, making animal noises and generally making a heck of a racket throughout our performance. We were not happy. However, the following day there was a knock at our hotel suite door and a Norwegian naval officer was standing there, he removed his hat and bowed and then proceeded to apologise profusely for the behaviour of his table the night before, explaining that they were a submarine crew and had been stuck in their sub for several weeks and that it was their first night ashore in a long time and they simply got so plastered they were out of control. Having sobered up later and remembered what they had done, they had wanted to make amends by inviting us to Sunday lunch on board the submarine and he said they would be at the show again that evening, but this time would remain be sober and appreciative. They kept their word on both counts and on the Sunday we dined on their minute submarine with the Captain and other officers. We all sat around a very small table, elbow to elbow and enjoyed some sort of Scandinavian stew and were then given

On stage - Cromer

Cast of 'Seaside Special', Cromer

Eric Morecambe presentation, Anglia T.V.

a tour of the submarine, which didn't take long as it was so small.

The trip was interesting and we travelled from one town to another in Norway on small 20 seater planes, performing in Stavangar, Oslo, Boda, Tromso, Alesund, Narvik and the most northern town in the world, Hammerfest, where we were officially given membership of the Royal and Ancient Polar Bear Society and presented with certificates. We spent five days at the SAS Royal Hotel in Boda. Our first show there was at 1.30 am in the hotel disco. The manager had a dry ice machine which he insisted we make use of during our show. As previously mentioned we always did a costume change halfway through the act whilst performing the song Bridge Over Troubled Water. As Stephen sang the first verse on our first night, Sandy and I rushed into the dressing room to do our quick change and ran smack into a thick mist. At first we couldn't see a thing, then managed to make out the vague outline of one highly embarrassed disco manager standing on top of the dry ice machine in a useless bid to stop the thick white mist from coming out of the top (it should have been passing through a tube in the wall and floating gently about the lower part of the stage). Instead both he and the entire room were engulfed and we could not see properly to change our clothes. We managed to get through it though and had a laugh about it later and thankfully, the manager decided to give up on that idea.

However our stay in Hammerfest proved to be the best part of our trip. The owner of the hotel where we performed, Gunner Larsson (a real character) and his wife Britt were as hospitable as could be and gave us a lovely time, showing us around and treating us really well.

On the whole the trip had been successful and fun, but two nights before the tour was due to finish we appeared in a disco/nightclub which was packed with people and the spotlights for the show instead of being suspended from the ceiling were placed on top of stands basically among the audience. Part way into the show the heaving audience managed to nudge one of the stands so that the light turned away slightly. This meant that for the second half of the show Sandy wasn't fully lit, but there was nothing we could do as no-one could have reached the stand to re-position it due to the mass of people, neither us or the club management. When we came off stage however, Sandy had gone into one of her strange moods and was furious with Stephen for not doing something about the light. Despite Stephen trying to reason with her about the difficulties, she just glared at him and stormed off. It was a really unpleasant scene but we assumed that the next morning she would have calmed down again. Not so, when Stephen knocked at our hotel room door she said she wanted her air ticket and she was going back to England. Stephen started to reason with her again and she actually hissed at him, then snatched his wrist bag off him assuming the tickets were in it, I then said "Oh for goodness' sake Sandy" and snatched it back, but before I could say anything else she drew back her arm and sent a straight right fist into my face, splitting my upper lip. I ran to the sink as blood was literally pouring out of my mouth which Sandy seemed oblivious to and still she didn't stop shouting at Stephen. I had to go to hospital and have stitches in my upper lip. When I returned to the hotel Stephen had rung the agent in England and Sandy had spoken to him and he had somehow persuaded her to stay and finish the last two nights of the tour. She still said nothing to me and I had to put up with the humiliation of appearing on stage that night with a fat lip. The show must go on of course, but it was the weirdest night. On the last day and all the way back to the U.K., Sandy never spoke once, not even to apologise or say anything like "I don't know what came over me" and when we got back home, she simply packed her things and went. We never saw her again.

So, time for another change….. but what? Stephen and I had some pictures taken as a duo and did a couple of local gigs while we pondered what to do next, then out of the blue I took a telephone call which would take us on another path altogether.

The call was from an American show promoter called Vince D'Amica who lived in the UK. Vince specialised in booking artistes to work on American bases throughout the world including some really big names, but he also had the rights to produce the Yogi Bear Show on American territory. He wanted to know if Stephen and I would join the cast of a Christmas package show which involved playing characters in a mini touring version of the Yogi Bear Show. The show was pre-recorded so the actors just mimed and was to be performed in the daytime for the service children, with the same cast performing their own cabaret acts in the evening for the adults. So the line up had to include vocalists, a comedian and dancers. I asked him if he had anyone else booked yet, he said no, so I found myself saying with total confidence "we can sort all that out, you pay us a fee and we will put the show together for you". He was really pleased with that idea, but I hadn't yet discussed it with Stephen, so I just hoped he was going to go for it too. Thankfully Stephen thought it was a great idea, and that was the start of the Flame Show and a happy and lucrative association with the agent Vince D'Amica. That show also heralded 1980 as one of the busiest and best in our careers.

Chapter 9
THE FLAME SHOW

It was a certainly challenge as the tour cast had to be put together quickly and then rehearsed for the Yogi Bear Show and an evening cabaret, which meant Stephen and I had to find three more girl dancers to work with us, who then had to have costumes made and be choreographed. Fortunately we managed to persuade Linda to come and rejoin us just for this trip, singing and dancing the parts she already knew in our cabaret show and to play Boo Boo in costume in the kids show. We found two more local girl dancers and brought in comedian/trumpeter J.J. Stewart, who had his own very funny act for the cabaret who would play the Ranger in the Yogi show. I played Goldilocks as the show was loosely based on the Goldilocks and the three bears story, and Stephen played Yogi Bear.

We managed to put everything together in time and were driven by minibus via the ferry to Belgium, then toured U.S. bases in Germany and Italy, returning home again for Christmas Eve. These shows went really well, though it was strange miming the parts in the Yogi show. As Goldilocks, I had to put up with a lot of rather rude gestures led by J.J. and the rest of the cast in the wings when I had to lip sync to such lines as "I can't possibly sit on this – it's much too hard" and, on finding daddy bears bed "Oh this is much too big! ", they continually tried to make me corpse with laughter, but I battled on. Vince was really pleased with how both the shows were received and said he could give us more work on the U.S. bases performing our cabaret show with the line up of Stephen with four girls. Stephen and I were keen although we knew it could take some time as we needed to find three more permanent girl singer/dancers, produce more costumes and music which all had to be recorded and really create a whole new show. We advertised in the Stage newspaper for dancers who could also sing, rented space in a studio at Pineapple in London and auditioned the dancers, literally dozens of dancers turned up for the auditions, it was a tough job narrowing them down to three. Eventually, when felt we had found the right people, publicity photos were taken, more backing tapes produced, rehearsal rooms rented, new costumes designed and made until we were happy with the finished act. Luckily we found that agents were really interested in the new line up including Don Jones who we had worked for in Norway, on that last fateful tour. He booked us for Norway again. But first we went out to the Middle East.

We spent a month in cabaret at the Infinity Club, in the Grundy Hotel in Bahrain, which was very successful and enjoyable and where we made good friends, we then went on to Cairo for four weeks at another hotel.

In the Cairo hotel we encountered a problem. We always had it written into our contract that we would be accommodated in rooms in the hotel, but on arrival found that we were taken to the top of the building where Stephen was shown the only proper bedroom reserved for artistes, but then we four girls were taken up another staircase into what can only be described as a large wooden shack that had been erected on the roof with four beds in it! I was furious, Stephen and I went to see the hotel owners, who said the hotel was fully booked and they could not give us another room. After much heated discussion, they agreed to put more furniture, somewhere to hang our clothes, bedside tables, lights, fans and so forth into this space to make it more habitable and said they would move us into rooms if any became available – somehow this was hard to believe, but we could only hope. Well we got the wardrobes and lights etc., but of course, though we continued to ask throughout our stay, the owner always made out that no hotel rooms were available.

Apart from this discomfort, the main road outside the hotel was really noisy. The traffic started to get busy from about 4 o'clock in the morning and everyone sounded their car horns, incessantly. With wooden walls, this was really annoying.

One of the girls was a keen horse rider and said she would like to find somewhere where she could go riding. We all fancied that idea and on making enquiries, found the AA Riding Stables near the pyramids at Giza. So we all went out for a hack in the desert which was wonderful and so peaceful after the chaotic noise of Cairo, so we came to a deal with the stables owner, that for a set fee we could come any day and ride into the desert. This we did on most days and the peace and quiet definitely restored the equilibrium, although the silence was broken unceremoniously one afternoon by my horse farting very loudly - funny how that can break the spell. We did develop a slight problem with the young owner of the stables who was constantly trying to chat up one or the other of us, offering cheap jewellery as an incentive to fall for his charms, but no-one went for it, so he just gave up in the end.

The hacks across the silent desert were really calming and enjoyable. One day however, we rode out in fine weather, then all of a sudden there was a distinct change in the atmosphere and as we began to head back a great sandstorm began. By the time we got back to the stables the poor horses and us were covered from head to foot in sand. Despite having scarves around our heads and wrapped over our faces and wearing sun glasses, the sand was stuck firmly on our skin, in our hair, our clothes – everywhere. It took about three days of showers and scrubbing to finally get rid of it all.

We did have a couple of great outings with friends we met from USAF, who took us on their bus on a tour along the banks of the River Nile and to Memphis, originally the capital of ancient Egypt where we saw the Steppes pyramid. It was always good to get out of the noisy city.

The girls and I were also asked by a top hairdressing salon in Cairo to be among the models at a big hairdressing show to take place at the Sheraton Hotel. The show was all set to funky music and we took turns to be models for a team of hairdressers, having a new style created then dancing along a catwalk. It was great fun and well attended and at the end of the evening hundreds of balloons were released from the ceiling – just like New Year's Eve.

Our shows took place in the hotel's nightclub and went very well, and occasionally, although not in our contract, we gave an extra performance in the hotel disco if it was very busy. On our final night, we had finished our show and packed up our costumes, removed our make up and were just about to go off to bed when there was a knock at the dressing room door and a member of the staff told us the owner wanted us to do another show in the disco. This management had taken real liberties with our contract and I'm afraid I was suddenly consumed by a red mist and promptly hit the roof. I started by saying we had completed our engagement, and our costumes were now packed away and if they wanted another show (which was not in our contract) they should have asked us earlier, but then the frustration we had all felt over our shack on the roof boiled up to the surface and I found myself also berating the poor man about the conditions we had been living in when we should have had hotel rooms and so on...... Meanwhile quite a crowd of hotel employees had gathered to watch this spectacle in awe. The distraught man left to relate all this to his boss while the girls were cheering and patting me on the back, a short time later there was another knock at the door and two porters were there saying they had come for our bags as the boss had instructed them to take them outside. We were being ejected from the hotel. Stephen then felt he should go and try to pour oil on these troubled waters and went off to speak to the owner. He eventually reappeared having successfully persuaded him, I don't know how, to allow us to sleep in the hotel that night and there was no more talk of an extra show. As we were due to fly back to the U.K. in the morning the girls all said they would have been quite prepared to sleep on the pavement outside as it had been worth it to see me saying what we all felt.

Our next trip, in complete contrast, was back to Norway where we stayed in proper guest rooms at a lovely hotel in a picturesque and peaceful spot in Tananger. We appeared in the hotel disco for several nights and also performed at a big naval base there. These shows went well, we all enjoyed ourselves and really appreciated the cleanliness and fresh air after Cairo.

Vince booked us again to tour U.S. bases in Germany and Italy, hard work but fun and we always went down a storm with the American audiences. This time, when we were in Naples we went on a trip to Pompeii and I was surprised at how much of the ancient city could still be seen.

Though I found the white remains of people and animals locked in volcanic larva forever pretty gruesome.

That year we spent the summer season in the Algarve, Portugal appearing at the casinos in Praie de Rocha, Villamoure and Monte Gordo, we would play one week in each and move on to the next then repeat the three again. Portugal was warm, with lovely beaches, great shopping and was also cheap to live. The girls were a bit put out though that in the six weeks we were there, no-one asked them out on a date. Then someone told them why. The fact was that wages were so low in Portugal that no local boys could afford to take out girls who were earning probably at least twice as much as they were. So, lovely as it was, eventually a bit of boredom was setting in. There being only so much sunbathing, eating and shopping to fill in the time anyone can take. The agent we were working for out there wanted us to go onto Madeira, which I would have loved, but sadly we couldn't accept as we had a T.V. show booked back home in the U.K.

The T.V. show was called "Up For The Cup" in which football clubs would choose a team of four acts each who had been popular with their supporters club audiences, to represent them. Each week two teams would battle it out via these artistes for the highest marks and a panel of four celebrities would mark each act and one act would be chosen by their sponsor to receive double marks. We were invited to appear on behalf of Southampton F.C. Supporters Club as we were very popular at that venue, along with three other acts chosen by the club and in a pleasing vote of confidence were selected by Southampton as their double mark hope. The host of the programme was "Diddy" David Hamilton.

We really enjoyed the day at the studios and David Hamilton sat down and chatted with us during our break between rehearsals and the actual show.

Despite our act getting the highest marks on the show and having that total doubled, another act on our team – a female impersonator - proved rather unpopular, and scored low marks, so Southampton just lost out to the other team, but as an act we could hold our heads high. Unfortunately we missed seeing the show aired as we were off abroad again, this time to Dubai in the United Arab Emirates for a month, but with new personnel.

Because Stephen and I employed the other three singer/dancers, the line up sometimes changed, but we had one girl who had been with us almost from the start of Flame, a beautiful blonde haired girl called Elaine who, despite not having been trained, was a natural dancer and was also able to choreograph. Just prior to going to Dubai we enlisted Carol who had done the very first Flame show/Yogi tour with us and was a superb dancer and her friend Penny, who Carol (rightly) recommended, as they had just finished a summer season's dancing contract at the Winter Gardens in Margate. This line up proved to be the best, most successful and probably the happiest group of all of the "Flame" period.

The Dubai Marine was a medium sized hotel with a cabaret room on the top floor and a wine bar run by a Brit – Brian Wilkes - called Wilkie's Wine Bar on the ground floor ably assisted by his friend "Chalky" White. We were given a warm welcome at the hotel and the rooms, service and food were all first class. Because Carol and Penny were still learning some of our numbers, we spent the first two days in heavy rehearsal, so they would know the full programme, but they were dedicated professionals and quick learners. On the third day though, the agent Rob Smith took us all out in his very large American car, along with his dog, to the beach which was beautiful, with warm crystal clear water. But we found that we could only cope with the extreme heat for about one and a half hours that first time. We also had a little trouble with stomach bugs during our stay, worst hit was Penny, who contracted some form of dysentery and had to be given injections by the doctor, which then gave her bad side effects, though she only had to miss one performance, and Carol and Elaine, really showed how professional they were by swapping some dancing roles and carrying on, with a woman down. However, apart from this, we had a wonderful month. We pulled in the crowds, made lots of friends and had a great social life there and even bumped into dance group Chantelle again who arrived a couple of days before we left to appear at another hotel in the town.

We went to three different beaches during our stay and I actually learned to water ski in the Creek. As I am aqua-phobic, this was a real feat for me, aided by the fact that Dubai Creek is particularly saline making it easier for nervous swimmers like me to keep afloat. My first attempt ended up with me being dragged through the water and getting half the creek up my nose, but Brian Wilkes said it was only because the boat towing me was not going fast enough and persuaded me to try again. On the third attempt I was up and stayed up for about half a mile – I screamed with delight. I was so pleased with myself.

By the time we left, Carol and Penny had perfected all the numbers and we had a new set of costumes made by a local tailor as we knew we would not be home for some time. Just before we left I was interviewed by a reporter from one of the Gulf newspapers for an article planned for their Sunday supplement, which sadly we never got to see as were in South Korea when it came out.

Vince D'Amica was coming over to meet us as he had been arranging further tours of U.S. bases for us in South Korea and the U.S.A. and also he wanted to meet some of the agents/show promoters in Dubai as he had lots of possible work in the Far East which became more viable if artistes could stop off and work in the Emirates en route. This would help with travel costs and journey times.

Whilst in Dubai I found to my horror that my passport was due to expire in four months time and I needed six clear months left on it in order to enter the United States. Brian came to my rescue and took me to see a friend of his at the British Embassy. Within ten minutes of my arrival, I had a new ten year passport. Quickest service ever!

On our nights off we would try to see other British acts appearing in Dubai including an English girl group called "Blonde Feeling", one of whom we already knew as she had worked in summer season in Margate, so we all had a good laugh and a catch-up.

When Vince arrived Stephen took him around Dubai and introduced him to various people who might be useful to him. It was an ideal situation then, but trouble was brewing in the Middle East and pressure would be put on the rulers in the Emirates not to allow hotels to book glamorous Western female acts, though we didn't know it at the time, this convenient route to the Far East would soon be closed to acts like ourselves.

The original plan with Vince was for us to go to Japan then on to South Korea, but for some reason to do with visas this had to be changed and so the Korean dates were brought forward. However this meant we would have a week to spare when our contract finished in Dubai before we were due to fly to Korea, so Vince arranged a deal with the luxurious Marbella Club in Sharjah for us to stay there for a week in exchange for performing just two shows on the Friday and Saturday night.. The Marbella Club was fabulous, we had two super luxurious villas and use of the pool and all other amenities on the site which included a cinema, though no-one was interested in sitting in the dark watching films with all that glorious sunshine.

The first show was by the pool in the evening and was very well attended. The problem was, due to the humidity and us performing a very high energy show outside , a lethal layer of moisture had formed on the surface of the platform on which we were dancing, which meant we were slipping all over the place and by the time we finished the spot we were all wringing wet and our hair was stuck to our faces, we looked and felt pretty awful despite the show going down very well with the audience.

Two members of that audience who really enjoyed our show invited us all out to lunch the following day. They were two businessmen who were great friends – even though one was Iranian and the other Iraqi, they joked about it though saying, they had been friends for years and always would be. The lunch was really enjoyable and it's always nice to be appreciated.

After our difficulties with the first show, the following night the management put carpeting over the stage and only removed it at the last moment before we went on, which at least solved the slipping problem and once again the audiences were thoroughly enthusiastic and appreciative.

As we only had to perform on those two nights, we were able to go back over to the Dubai Marine to watch the new show there which comprised our old friend J.J. Stewart and a British female act called the Nitebirds. We invited J.J. over to a pool day at the Marbella Club with us, to soak up some sun and luxury and have a catch up, fun times.

Brian also invited us out to a barbecue party on an island in the Creek one day, not as picturesque as the originally planned location – the beach at Hamrya – which had been closed to the public as it was apparently full of soldiers keeping an eye out for troublesome Iranians, but there was plenty to eat and drink, music and boats for water skiing and we had a real laugh.

The night before we left the Marbella Club we decided not to go to bed, but have a bit of a party with all our friends around the pool. We had such a wonderful time over those five weeks and had made so many friends, we were sad to leave and really hoped to return, but due to religious "politics" in the Middle East, that unfortunately would not happen. We left at 7 a.m. to catch the 9.30 am flight to Bahrain where we were to connect with a flight to Seoul via Bangkok, which fortunately wasn't departing until 3.30 pm in the afternoon, because Vince managed to miss the first flight due to being held up on a lengthy telephone call. We were very relieved to see him arrive in time for the next flight. We landed in Seoul, which was six hours ahead of Dubai time at 11 am and booked in at the Sheraton Walker Hill Hotel near the airport and after a rest were taken by Vince to the American Services restaurant to eat, then went back in time to watch a spectacular show at the Sheraton. The first half was a Korean spectacular, performed on a fantastic stage which at one point showed a mirror image in which we could see 25 girls in Korean national costume all playing drums, then we realised they were actually descending from the ceiling. In another scene a boat appeared on stage filled with singers and musicians while girls in stunningly beautiful costumes danced around it. The second half was a western floor show with an Australian/French production company which had fabulous choreography. They had motorbikes on stage in their opener, a 'space craft' came down during a second show number, followed by a voodoo themed dance routine which concluded with an "earthquake," and for a finale, two massive crystal chandeliers descended into the auditorium with a singer on each one. The whole show was breathtaking. Afterwards, we met a few of the Australian dancers and they wished us well and warned us that we probably wouldn't get any sleep for a few days. We laughed at this and said we were pretty exhausted and nothing would keep us awake, but they said it happens to everyone when they first come here – and it turned out they were right.

Although the Sheraton Walker Hill was a great hotel, it was outside of the town, so the next day we moved into the more central Crown Hotel and, as there was a curfew in Seoul at the time – no-one allowed on the streets after 10 p.m. - was a much better location for us.

Just as the Aussie dancers had predicted, it took us all variously between four and six nights before we actually slept despite having comfortable beds. Although there was always a weird garlicky aroma which seeped through the air vents in the en suite bathrooms, due to the Korean habit of making and storing pots of fermented Kimchi in or just outside their kitchens. The smell must have travelled through the pipe system into the hotels bathrooms, but after a while, we just got used to it.

The hotel was within walking distance of Etaiwon, the amazing shopping area, which basically held the outlet shops for all the fashionable clothes and goods manufacturers in Seoul. The bargains were astounding. Also on Etaiwon was a Korean owned American style breakfast café where we ate breakfast most mornings. Our other meals were eaten at various American service men's clubs and restaurants, though we did once decide to eat a late supper in the hotel restaurant. Because of the curfew, we always had to be back in the hotel by 10 p.m. and we were the only people in the restaurant when suddenly things rather came alive – a large rat ran down one of the curtains and another popped up out of a vase and proceeded to scurry about the carpet searching for food. We went to reception where Stephen tried to report to the staff the fact that there were rats running about in the restaurant. They spoke no English at all and while Stephen got more and more frustrated trying to explain and galvanise someone into action, they just stood and grinned at us. So we eventually gave up, but decided to stay out of the restaurant in the evenings from then on.

We spent quite a lot of time shopping in Etaiwon and I bought a wonderful new suitcase with a silk lining, pockets, tough zips and wheels and straps for the princely sum of £8, throwing my other suitcase away, and proceeded to fill it with jeans at £4 per pair, £2 embroidered sweaters, gadgets and gifts for friends and family for Christmas. I bought my mum an eel skin bag and purse for about £20 (which I later saw in Macey's department store in New York selling for $200 U.S.). I also bought a pair of white "moon" boots which it turned out were just about to be the next big fashion trend in the U.K. and U.S.A.. All the goods were so cheap. Stephen possessed a beautiful silk shirt that he had paid a lot of money for in England, which he took in to a Korean tailor who then made six more exact copies in silks of different colours for him for about £6 each. Finally, as we felt 1980 was a year when we were virtually travelling round the world, we had five bomber jackets made with "Flame World Tour 1980" embroidered on them. Stephen's was red with white embroidered writing and ours were white with red writing.

The shows were going smoothly in the U.S. forces clubs apart from the occasional electricity malfunction. On one occasion when we four girls were singing "Stop In The Name Of Love" the power suddenly dropped and because we had taped backing tracks, the tape slowed down and dropped a tone and so of course did we, having no other choice, it then suddenly went back up and we were back to normal speed. That was quite amusing, but the second blip with power happened on another night when we were performing a medley of songs from James Bond films and had reached the part in "Live and Let Die" where Elaine and Penny have a choreographed fight with a whip and a knife. Suddenly the power just went off leaving the girls poised with weapons aloft and Stephen, Carol and myself mute behind the microphones. There was nothing for it but to leave the stage until the power came back on.

One day Vince told us he had arranged for Flame to be guest artistes on the South Korean Song Contest which was being televised in Seoul. We were to sing three songs in the guest spot while the judging was taking place. We were very happy to do this and found the T.V. studios in quite a state of chaos with all the various acts and bands milling about everywhere. The T.V. company gave us lunch and we met several of the acts before going on stage for our spot which went really well with the live audience, but then we had to leave in order to get ready for the evening's show and thought no more about it.

We had no idea then that the Korean Song Festival which would air on T.V. the following night would be seen by about 20 million viewers throughout the Far East and Australasia. So on the morning following the programme (which we never saw as we were out working), having decided to risk breakfast at the hotel for a change, couldn't help noticing that a rather large crowd of hotel staff was gathering about the room and watching us. This was strange. We put it down to the possibility that we had not eaten breakfast there before. After we went out to a shopping mall and noticed people were running out of shops to look at us and point. Again, we hadn't a clue why. But it was when we all squeezed into a large taxi in the late afternoon to be driven to the club we were due to appear that night, that all fell into place. We were about halfway to the club, when the driver suddenly stood on the brakes almost throwing us all into the front seat. We thought something must be in the road, but the driver suddenly started shouting excitedly "Oh, I know who you are! You are Flame from the Song Festival" then he got on his radio and shouted excitedly to whoever was listening, before handing us his worksheet attached to a clipboard which he asked us all to autograph. He was totally oblivious to the fact he was causing a traffic hold up, as he had stopped in the middle of the road, but eventually he calmed down and drove us on to the club grinning from ear to ear and apparently thrilled to bits.

Looking back, following our appearance on the Korean Song Festival, in the Far East at least, we could have been famous......

However, it was almost time to move on and Vince gathered us together to say that there would be a three day gap before we needed to be in Monterey, California to start work at our first venue and as we would have to enter the United States via Hawaii – could we talk it over and let him know whether we would like to have our three days off in Korea or leave and spend them in Hawaii. There was of course no need for a discussion, just a united "Hawaii!" and so at the end of our two week stay in Korea we flew out to Honolulu and were driven to a super hotel overlooking Waikiki Beach. We thought we were in heaven.

We spent quite a bit of time on Waikiki beach, but also hired a car for a day in order to explore other parts of the main island. We drove into the country, enjoyed a good look around and stopped for a while on a high cliff top where the flora was lush and tropical from which we had a superb view of the surfers beneath.

One of the most striking features of Honolulu was its magnificent sunsets. On our last evening Carol, Elaine and I were sitting on the beach at sundown and I was taking photographs when a couple holding hands came into view on the horizon, silhouetted against the sunset and we realised it was Stephen and Penny. Romance had blossomed on that tour and I'm pleased to say they are still together more than 35 years later. Unfortunately most of the photos we took were spoilt in the x-ray machines at one of the airports.

The night before we flew from Hawaii to Los Angeles, I telephoned my aunt Marie who lived there with her husband Jerry and we made arrangements to meet up once we were settled in a hotel.

We flew into the very "space age" L.A. airport and proceeded to choose a hotel just for that night from the many advertised on the information board at the airport, settling on a motel which was not too far away and advertised a courier service that would pick us up. The motel was fine and it had a coffee shop out front, so I rang Marie and Gerry to come over and meet us there. When I gave them the address they sounded a little reticent, but turned up anyway and we had a great catch up, but they spent a lot of time glancing over their shoulders and informed us that this was a rather dubious area and that most of the other diners in the coffee shop were prostitutes and their pimps! However, no-one bothered us and the motel rooms were clean and comfortable, so after a good night's sleep, we were met by a lovely guy called Ted who was to be our driver for the week on this part of the trip. Ted had a "pimped up ride" in the form of a customised mini bus with plush carpeted interior, blue curtains at the windows, comfortable seating and little round tables for drinks which he kept in the built in fridge. First we were taken to our motel for the week in Monterey – the Magic Carpet Lodge, named after the red flowering plant which literally carpeted much of the landscape. It was the end of October, but still very hot in California and the motel had a swimming pool, plus an excellent coffee shop. Over the week we appeared in various clubs on the military base there for officers, sergeants and enlisted men and the shows were really well received. One night, a star act appeared on the base in the form of Billy Paul and his backing band. His biggest hit was "Me and Mrs Jones" which when he performed it in the club went on for a good ten minutes, in fact he only sang a few songs which each lasted a long time with improvisation. His young backing group also stayed in the motel, so it was nice to have a chat and a laugh with them.

In the daytime, our driver Ted took us out sightseeing and we went to the attractive new town of Carmel where Clint Eastwood was the mayor and had a restaurant called the Hog's Breath, (sadly we didn't bump into him, much to Carol's disappointment as she was a huge fan). We drove past the star studded homes on17 mile drive up to Pebble Beach, where we saw the famous lone Cypress and "ghost" trees (trees that had died and petrified, turning them completely white) and enjoyed feeding the tame Prairie dogs that lived among the rocks overlooking the bay where two tides met. Finally ending the day with a visit to the quaint old fisherman's wharf where old warehouses had been converted to shops and cafes and the main attraction was an enormous fairground carousel with beautiful horses, which we just had to ride on.

At the end of the week, Major Clemens who was in charge of the clubs, invited us all to his super home set among towering Redwood pines for a barbecue to thank us. Not that we needed to be thanked, we were having a blast.

From the heat of California we flew on to Denver, Colorado which was a little cooler but nevertheless still sunny when we arrived. It was also one mile above sea level and the air was thinner there. We had been booked to appear at the airmen's club on the USAF training base. Our first night was definitely well received, in fact the audience, who were very young guys, cheered and whistled all the way through our performance, this enthusiastic response was very welcome as the thin air was making us slightly breathless during our solid hour of non-stop singing and dancing with fast costume changes. We no longer had our lovely driver Ted, so we hired a car and went for a drive up into the Rocky Mountains, enjoying stunning scenery and exploring some of the old gold mining towns which had been preserved. We also visited Buffalo Bill's Memorial Museum and his grave.

We had planned to make another trip later in the week however a radical change in the weather put paid to that idea when thick snow arrived overnight and in the morning we noticed all the local drivers had fitted chains to their tyres, which we did not have. The moon boots bought in Seoul came in very useful for the snowy conditions though.

Before we appeared at the club, the sergeant in charge had very nervously called us into his office and explained to us that a blunder had been made and they had inadvertently booked two female groups to appear that week. Apart from ourselves they had also booked an all girl rock band and what's more we would need to share the only dressing room. He seemed terrified that there would be jealousy and trouble between the two sets of females. He didn't need to worry. The rock band called "Dreamer" and ourselves got on like a house on fire and as we weren't performing the same type of material there was no clash at all. They were very good musicians and we both went down a storm with the boys, so the club was packed every night. We did notice that the girls in Dreamer dressed in a very butch way at the start of the week, as though they had to prove they were as good as the guys at rockin' but by the end of the week they had more make up on, the vocalist had flowers in her hair and they had a more feminine look altogether, which was good to see as they made a great rock sound anyway, but could be proud to be female too.

When we were out and about in Denver, having spent the previous week among the mainly healthy looking Californians, we were amazed at how many really overweight and positively obese people we saw in Denver, and we noticed that nobody walked anywhere, people got into their cars just to drive around the corner.

We decided to go out to a bar one afternoon which was famous for its wonderful ice creams and I ordered an ice cream with hot fudge sauce which was divine. We all ordered an alcoholic drink too and were sitting enjoying our ice creams when the manager approached the table and asked me if I was over twenty-one (the minimum drinking age in the state), before I could respond all the girls began falling about, shrieking with laughter and I had to say to this bemused man "the reason they're laughing is I am the oldest here". The girls all starting nodding and I thanked him for the compliment (I was 33 at the time). The poor guy was so embarrassed and returned to the bar somewhat red in the face..

At the end of another great week, we flew off to Louisville, Kentucky known as the bluegrass state. This time we would be entertaining the U.S. Army but, apart from the shows, there wasn't so much in the area for us to enjoy. The General Patten Museum was there and there were tanks on display everywhere on the streets, but these didn't really appeal to us girls. We did drive past Fort Knox, the U.S. gold bullion depository., but they weren't giving out any free samples.

Soon it was time to return to England, but, as we had to fly to New York in order to get the plane home and the tickets were open, three of us decided to stay in New York for three more days just to see it before returning home. Carol and Elaine chose to fly back to the U.K. to see their families while Stephen, Penny and I stayed on in Manhattan and crammed as much as we could into that short time. We went up the Empire State building (at our second attempt, as visibility was too poor in the morning), saw the Statue of Liberty, visited the shops, including Macey's department store which had nine floors, fed the squirrels in Central Park and saw two shows, one on Broadway starring Mickey Rooney and Anne Miller called "Sugarbabes" where, as a bonus, we encountered ballet star Rudolf Nureyev in the foyer, he was wearing a long leather coat and sporting a floor length scarf (not unlike a Dr. Who outfit). We also saw the amazing Christmas show at Radio City Music Hall. The seats for this latter were either $8 or $11 and Stephen asked the man in the box office "what's the difference?" "Three dollars" came the deadpan reply. Worth every cent as the show was stunning, culminating in the most amazing nativity scene, with a stable containing Mary, Joseph and baby Jesus, real live animals, including camels, three shepherds, three wise men and, using all the hydraulics you could imagine, coming up from below stage and down from the rooftops, were a full orchestra, a vast choir of angels and finally a mighty Wurlitzer organ. Yes - over the top - but breathtaking too.

We flew home at the end of a fabulous and exciting year and within a couple of weeks were back in Europe doing another Yogi Bear Show and Cabaret on U.S. bases in Germany, Italy and Holland, this time we travelled in a luxurious coach owned by a great German guy called Reiner. Carol's fiancé Derry who played the trumpet was also with us. The story was different on this Yogi show and featured a 'guest appearance' from Fred Flintstone and Barney Rubble who had a dance duet. The two characters were played by Elaine (Fred) and myself (Barney) and we did a sort of soft shoe shuffle - well more of a soft foot shuffle as we had bare feet. Due to this fact and the temperature of the stage being very cold, on one occasion I suddenly got cramp in my toes and they seemed to lock together, causing me to have to stamp my foot a few times in an attempt to relieve the problem. The routine was perfectly choreographed, but suddenly went out of sync. and due to the fact that the giant heads made our vision limited to say the least, suddenly we were bumping into each other and the set routine went for a burton. Thankfully, I don't think the audience caught on as we were playing for comedy anyway.

We had fun performing the Yogi shows, but also had great success with our own cabaret as, having the same line up for a long period meant the show had become really tight and the Americans loved us and really appreciated the dancing and show numbers, sometimes applauding mid song when they really liked something.

We had high hopes for 1981 being as good if not better than 1980, but it proved to be rather up and down. The main problem being that the Emirates stopped booking acts with glamorous girls, in order to keep the peace with other Muslim countries in the Middle East and that really closed the gateway to South East Asia and, apart from work on the American bases, there was not much decent work to be had in Europe for our type of show, as so much of the entertainment scene on the continent verged on sleazy and pornographic clubs.

Stephen Gold with 'Flame' new girl Sandy

Our Margate Coffee Shop

Elaine and me as Fred and Barney

First incarnation of 'Flame' Show

Backstage at the Yogi Bear Show

Carole in Dubai

New line up for Stephen Gold with 'Flame'

Mum, Dad and Me on the Isle of Wight

Danny and the Juniors

My lovely horse in Giza, Eygpt

In the office of Solid Gold Promotions

'Dream' leaving Brize Norton for the Falklands

'Dream', Celia and RAF 202 Squadron,
South Atlantic

With Captain Black and his officers onboard
HMS Invincible

Bobby Knut, Carol, HRH Prince Andrew and me

Nidge and Ron Buckett's kitchen, Port Stanley

Celia's turn to be winched onto Tug Yorkshireman

Ready to leave Port Stanley (with handbag)

'Dream' in Dressing room, Port Stanley airfield

Official RAF Pin ups "Dream"

With lovely Lil in her showbiz bar

Celebrating David Hamilton's birthday

Penny and Carole - 'Poppy'

Me with Michael York

With Patricia Hodge on set of The Heat of The Day'.

Me with Sir Michael Gambon at Granada Studios

Chapter 10
SOLID GOLD PROMOTIONS

It was about this time that Stephen and I decided to start a company and called ourselves Solid Gold Promotions. We had already created and promoted the Flame Show, so decided we could promote and book other artistes and produce different shows. Also, living in a seaside resort with its Winter Gardens and Queen's Hall in the town, we felt we could put on one night shows at these venues instead of just trying to find work for ourselves.

We did take the Flame show to Cologne in Germany and appeared in a discotheque there which turned out to be good, so when we were asked to work in a theatre in Barcelona, we thought that would also be a good venue for us. We signed a contract to present two half hour sets on a bill with other artistes and because it was a theatre, we assumed all would be fine. On arrival at the theatre we did a sound check which went fine and then we were invited to sit and watch the other artistes rehearsing. One of these was a very mature Spanish lady vocalist who sang beautifully, until we noticed she was removing some of her clothing too, so then this woman who looked about sixty, finished her song topless. We were astonished and remembered what Angela and Mara in Portugal had told us about Spain expecting acts to be pornographic, but the undignified sight of this lady vocalist being reduced to having to strip when she sang, was truly sickening.

After the rehearsals, the agent came over to us and said the manager wanted us to appear several times throughout the show and perform one routine at a time like a dancers' chorus. We said an emphatic "No" pointing out that we were a complete act and they had signed a contract booking us to perform two half hour spots. The agent asked us to leave the matter with him and the argument continued with the manager who said if he didn't get his own way then he didn't want us at all. The signed contract didn't seem relevant as far as he was concerned. Stalemate. So that was that.

The agent however told us not to worry because he would get us some other work and we should stay in our apartment and wait for him to sort it out. In retrospect we should have cut our losses and got the next plane back, but he was a well known agent over in Spain and seemed plausible, so we stayed for another two weeks, paying for our own keep and calling the agent every day, eventually accepting that no other gig was going to be forthcoming, Stephen and I went to see a Spanish lawyer and showed him the contract. He said that as Spain had the same workers' contractual rights as the U.K, we had a case against the theatre management.

As we were by then convinced that the agent was not going to find us alternative work, we returned home. Stephen and I paid the girls two week's wages each anyway and after all the travel and accommodation costs we were around £3,000 out of pocket. I wrote to our union Equity and enclosed copies of the contract and all relevant documents including the name and address of the Spanish lawyer we had taken advice from and waited to hear how they could help us. After a couple of weeks, of hearing nothing, I telephoned Equity's legal department and was told they couldn't find our documents. So I re-sent them copies and this time Equity's legal department came back with the excuse that the Spanish agent had now left Barcelona and they couldn't locate him. I then personally set about finding his new address which was now in Madrid and promptly passed it on to Equity. Following this, they said that the theatre manager had told them he did not sign or recognise the signature on the contract, so he could not be held liable. We argued that someone had signed it and if it was the agent, he must be liable, but Equity just didn't get anywhere and we were left high and dry with a pretty bad taste in the mouth, total loss of faith in our union and a large hole in our bank balance.

However, we just had to get on with life and were soon off again to appear on American bases in Holland, Germany and Italy for Vince, successful as always especially the show in Holland on a co-occupied base which also had Canadian troops and their families who gave us an amazing standing ovation at the end of the evening.

We then went on to spend the summer season on the Isle of Wight. We took a large apartment in East Cowes for the summer and toured a variety of venues. Elaine had left the act by then, as she met a lovely guy who was road managing on a previous tour for Vince and they planned to get married. We were sorry to lose her, but we had a lovely replacement in the form of a dancer called Chris. Carol also was not with us that summer and another local girl dancer called Jackie who had worked with us before, completed the line up.

That was a good summer season and we sometimes went over to the mainland on the Red Funnel ferry to appear on Sunday concerts at resorts in the south of England with stars including Diana Dors and also Rolf Harris, who was lovely and showed no signs of the sexual predation that has him serving a prison sentence now.

I met a new boyfriend that summer, a civil engineer who was also working on a contract for the whole summer on the Island and he would sometimes come to our gigs.

Although there was not as much work all year round for our type of show, we found the Flame Show was in great demand for the Christmas and New years period.. So Stephen and I pulled out all the resources we had and in December we had three lots of personnel lined up as the Yogi/cabaret tour was booked again for the two weeks before Christmas for Germany, a hotel in India wanted the Flame show throughout Christmas and January and the casinos in the Algarve also wanted the show for New Years Eve, through January and early February. So Stephen and Penny took one line-up out to India, I was in charge of the Yogi/cabaret tour in Germany and Italy and our lead dancer Carol and her fiancé Derry took the third group to Portugal. Fortunately we had some friends in Margate, a married couple who sometimes worked as an acrobatic dance duo, but also had a dance group with whom they toured overseas and they had decided not to work at Christmas, so kindly helped us out with the loan of extra costumes.

I worked very hard up to the tour start date, taking charge of rehearsals with the new line up for both the cabaret and the Yogi Bear show. I engaged a male vocalist to sing Stephen's songs in the cabaret and play the ranger in the Yogi show, but I also needed someone to wear the Yogi Bear suit and double as a roadie/sound man for the evening shows. I tentatively asked my boyfriend if he would be interested and was genuinely surprised to find he was rather keen.

However by the time rehearsals began I had caught a cold and with all the extra work was getting pretty exhausted, so by the time we left on the tour bus, I was suffering badly with 'flu. On the coach journey over I felt absolutely rotten and must have looked looked pretty awful too. However, when we started the actual gigs I began to feel a lot better and as always, the shows went well. One evening when we had finished the gig, we boarded the tour bus to drive back to our lovely guest house which was only about a twenty minutes drive along the autobahn. Snow had been falling heavily all day and about halfway along the autobahn we came to a complete stop along with hundreds of other vehicles. We were there for most of the night. The driver could not keep the engine running all night, which meant no heater either and we were frozen. However, our spirits lifted when we saw the German Red Cross were coming to the rescue by driving along the hard shoulder and stopping every now and then to serve hot drinks. So we alighted from the cold bus into the even colder night air and queued for the hot tea, which turned out to be disappointingly tepid.. By then we were thoroughly chilled. Eventually in the early hours, after the snow drifts had been cleared enough, we were able to drive on, firstly as far as the next service area where there was a stampede for the toilets.

On arrival at the guest house however, our rosy faced country land lady was so shocked to hear our sorry tale that she sat us down for breakfast and not only brought us piping hot coffee but also insisted on adding a generous dollop of brandy into each cup free gratis, which was most welcome.

When that tour ended I remember getting thoroughly plastered on wine on the way back on the ferry home (a rare occurrence for me), as we initially decided to have a bottle of German wine with our meal, then someone suggested that we should perhaps continue with a bottle from France then, getting into our stride, an Italian wine, followed by another, possibly a Chilean. I have always been a giggler on the rare occasions I have been drunk, this being no exception as apparently I giggled unstoppably all the time we were in customs, before being assisted back on the tour bus and promptly passing out, I woke up when we arrived at my front door.

A few weeks after a Christmas break in Bournemouth with Jim, he and I broke up and I was pretty gutted at the time. But, always busy, I had to make a trip out to the Algarve to see how Carol and Derry's group were getting on and take them some replacement costumes as they would be repeating their shows, the system there, as I mentioned before, was to perform one week in each casino and then back to the first and do the same clubs again, which required some change of programme and outfits. I arrived the day before they were due go on to the third casino which was in Villamoure.

When we arrived there we found the villa which was allotted for the visiting show was in an awful state of dampness and peeling plaster. I was furious, though obviously the previous show had amazingly put up with it. So when the group arrived at the casino to start rehearsing, Derry and I went straight up to the Manager's office. He was having a meeting at the time, but I wasn't prepared to wait. I told him about the state of the property and that it was not fit for habitation, explaining that the mattresses were damp and the bathroom ceiling had great clumps of plaster hanging down. I could see that I was going to be fobbed off, so I just stood my ground and refused to leave his office until he agreed to do something about it, pointing out that if the group slept there, there was every chance they would become ill and not be able to appear anyway, so doing something about it would be in his interest too. I am pleased to say that after sending someone to inspect the villa and arranging workers to go in to re-plaster the walls and ceilings, dry out the place and replace the mattresses, he did arrange for us to stay in a large suite at the Golf Hotel for a couple of nights, while the work was being done.

Carol also had another concern though - she suspected one of the new dancers had bulimia, this girl would sit down and eat with the others, but liked to pour vinegar all over her food, then they would later hear her throwing up in the bathroom. Carol had talked to her about this but, although admitting that she had suffered with bulimia once in the past, she totally denied it was happening again. So on my return to England, I had to telephone her parents (who were both G.P.s), to let them know and they confirmed that she had suffered with Bulimia in the past, but they thought she had fully recovered, so my news must have been upsetting for them and it was also a bit of a headache for Carol, but the dancer got through the remainder of the shows without falling ill and then went home to her parents. We did not use her again, but I hope she recovered.

As some of the best work for our type of act was sadly beginning to dry up, Stephen and I decided to use our experience to develop Solid Gold Promotions having decided to put shows on ourselves and we also arranged to take American artistes who were touring for Vince and give them one night bookings at the Queen's Hall in Margate, including The Floaters with Sugar and Danny and the Juniors (minus Danny) who had a major hit with "At the Hop" some twenty years before. The show with the Juniors was a great night, Stephen and some of his local musician friends got together to form a support band playing good old rock n'roll, with Penny and Carol in bobby socks, flared skirts and pony tails dancing. On the night, we had the bonus of a large group in the audience who turned up in "rockers" outfits, teddy boys in drapes and drainpipes and girls in enormous skirts with petticoats, and had brought a variety of records by the Juniors to have the covers signed. The Juniors were three Italian brothers who put on an excellent show with superb harmonies and tight choreography and the evening was a great success.

We also had a lot of fun with the Floaters (who had a big hit in the U.K. with a song called "Float On"). Originally a four piece all male group, they now also featured a female singer by the name of Sugar. I had arranged for them to stay at the best hotel in Broadstairs, but after their rehearsal I took them across the road to a sea front guest house owned by Mrs Lily Cox. 'Lil' as she was known, had a basement bar that was frequented by most of the artistes who appeared at the Winter Gardens, the walls were totally covered with photos of them all and she was a lovable Scottish lady who everyone liked. Lil fussed around the Floaters, giving them tea and scones after which the group took me to one side and said – "we want to stay here, forget the posh hotel, we like it here with Lil". So I had to cancel the rooms at the big hotel and thankfully didn't get caught out with a cancellation fee, and the Floaters moved in to Lil's sea front guest house. I had put together a small dance group of three girls led by Carol and called them Dream and they went on as a support to the Floaters. After the show we all went over to Lil's and ended up dancing the night away with the Floaters and Sugar in her show biz bar downstairs. It was a really fun night.

By then, we had so many attractive girl singers and dancers on our books, that I also found work for them doing promotions and fashion modelling. That was my side of the business and I regularly booked models for Riceman's Department Store in Canterbury which put on fashion shows all year round. I had to undercut London agency fees, but found that the girls all seemed to like working for me and were happy to come down to Canterbury, where the store always treated them well.

Stephen also came up with the idea of staging an event at the Queen's hall to promote holiday companies, a sort of exhibition, but featuring live entertainment as well.

He secured some big holiday names such as the Cunard liner Q.E.2 to participate and we staged appropriate live performances such as flamenco dancing to promote Spain and also presented a fashion show featuring clothes from a rather swish boutique in Cliftonville.

I organised and commered the fashion show and a few days before the event I took five attractive models including Elaine who used to work for us, over to the boutique in my car. My Renault 12 only sat five people at best and there were six of us, so I was praying I wouldn't get stopped by the police. After the selection and trying on of the clothes, we were returning to Margate in the car and as I pulled up to stop at traffic lights, a police motorcyclist also stopped at the side of us, he looked into the car, signalled me to wind down the window and said "Can you get any more in there?" and before I could stop myself I replied "Oh I'm sure we could squeeze you in somewhere officer." The girls burst into spontaneous laughter, the policeman went bright red and I bit my lip. But the lights changed and he shot straight off and amazingly I got away with it.

That summer, Stephen put on a show in Jersey for the season there, but I chose not to be involved, apart from costuming the dancers and going over for a week to make sure the costumes were all o.k. for the final rehearsal and first night, after which I returned to Margate to look after the business at home.

One of the shows I booked for the Queens Hall was a football forum featuring Bobby Moore and Geoff Hurst heroes of the 1966 World cup winning England squad, and chaired by Kenny Lynch. I met the guys when they arrived, though I already knew Kenny having worked with him and Jimmy Tarbuck several times, and took them into the Queen's Hall at the Winter Gardens to set up. The first half of the evening consisted of the forum where members of the audience could ask questions of Bobby Moore and Geoff Hurst, humorously fielded by Kenny. The second half featured a film put together of fifty golden goals, which gave the guys a break, after which they returned to the stage for a final session. Whilst the goal film was showing and they were having a drink in the bar and I asked them if, before returning home they would like to pop over to Lil's bar to have a nightcap, this idea was met with great enthusiasm. So, following the show and bit of autograph signing on their part, I took them across and rang the front door bell at Lil's. Her cockney husband Ted answered the door and went positively delirious with joy at the sight of Bobby Moore standing on his doorstep. As he showed them down to the bar he was raving on to Bobby Moore about the photo that had become famous of him kissing the World Cup in 1966.

There were just a small group of guest house residents in the bar who were pretty amazed when they saw who had just turned up, but the guys were really affable and friendly with everyone. Geoff Hurst only had one pint as he was driving, but Bobby Moore had two or three before they left, promising Ted that he would send him a signed copy of that photo. Meanwhile Kenny who had lost his driving license at the time, stayed on, missing his train home in the process and became very merry indeed, playing Lil's piano and singing loads of cockney songs with the night turning into a real "knees up" into the wee small hours, by which time he was pretty much legless and there was nothing else for it but to take him back to the house in Westbrook and, despite him trying to fall asleep along the bench seat at the kitchen table, saying "I shall be fine here", I managed to help him up the stairs and put him into Stephen's bed for the night (Stephen being in Jersey at the time). The next morning when I cooked him some breakfast, Kenny, now sober, said he was really grateful and any time he could return the favour I only had to ask. Whilst having breakfast the doorbell rang, I had forgotten it was my cleaner's morning to come. She was a jolly woman with learning difficulties and on seeing Kenny tucking into bacon and eggs, pointed her finger at him and just kept repeating "oh, oh, oh." I helped her out by saying "Kenny Lynch" then added "all the 'lardies' come here for breakfast" which sent cockney Kenny into a fit of laughter.

The following day I had a call from an ecstatic Ted to say that he had just received the signed photo from Bobby Moore of him kissing the world cup. He was over the moon. So nice that Bobby Moore kept his word.

Earlier in the year, I was asked by the owners of a very smart restaurant venue called the Tudor House in Maidstone, if I could arrange for them to have a guest Radio Disc Jockey to appear at the opening of their new disco. Remembering David Hamilton as a really pleasant guy, I contacted his P.A. and asked about booking him. David, it turned out had friends in Maidstone that he could stay with and was keen to do the gig. So he came down and was astonished to find it was me who had booked him as he remembered talking to me when we did the "Up For The Cup" programme. The owners of the Tudor House were a generous couple and gave David and his friends a steak dinner with wine, David asked me to sit with them and we carried on talking, until it was time for him to go on. At the end of the evening to my surprise David asked if he could see me again, but I courteously said no and explained that I was still feeling pretty cut up over my split with my last boyfriend at the time, but David gave me his card anyway and said if any time I was in London, to give him a ring and perhaps we could meet up for a meal.

Chapter 11
CAROLE ST. JAMES AND DREAM

The owners of the Tudor house said they would also like to have cabaret shows on Saturday nights and so asked me to sort that out for them too, and I decided it would be a good regular booking for the dance act Dream which had Carol from the Flame show and two younger local girls, with myself as singer and commere, along with a featured cabaret act and so we began to work regularly on Saturday nights there.

I sometimes had to go up to London to buy fabrics for new stage costumes and so the next time I needed to get some, I decided I would give David a call as he had asked, not sure if he would remember. To my surprise, he seemed thrilled that I had called and suggested we meet up after my shopping trip and go and watch his team Fulham play. I thought "why not" so that's what we did and after the match he did take me for a meal in a very nice restaurant but, not what one would call a romantic meal for two, as the entire Fulham team came too. I have to admit, we really got on well together, so over the next few months I would often see him in London and David would sometimes come to Margate, even helping me dig up my potatoes in the garden one day. As he played football for the Showbiz 11 team, I also accompanied him on some of their match days too.

During this time I contacted Combined Services Entertainment again, the Flame show had been too large a group to work for them, but Dream was a better option and Derek Agutter (father of actress Jenny) was keen to use us. The Falklands war began on the 2nd April 1982 when Argentina invaded the Falkland Islands and the British sent a task force to take the islands back. It ended when the Argentinians surrendered 74 days later in June, so Derek said there would likely be a request to send a show out there in the future, but not until the airport was open again on Port Stanley and asked if I would be interested. I said I definitely would, assuming at the time that it would be weeks ahead. But the call came a lot sooner than expected as the Royal Navy put in a special request to CSE for a small show to be put together despite knowing that it could not be an official CSE show and saying that they would take total responsibility for it, as there were ships out there with both navel and other troops on who had been away from home much longer than they normally would because of the war and morale was low. A show was what they needed and they couldn't wait for the airport to reopen for an official tour to be put together.

When he rang, Derek Agutter explained all this to me and said he would prefer to send someone like me as I had a lot of experience of CSE shows and knew the ropes, (including expected codes of behaviour off stage) and asked if we would still be willing to go. I said I would talk to the girls about it and get back to him as soon as possible. But I had two problems, unfortunately one of the dancers was only 17 years of age which meant she would have to stay behind as the minimum age was 18, plus we had an agreement with the Tudor House to appear there on Saturday nights.

As it turned out, the owners of the Tudor House were really pleased for us and willing to release us from the contract for a month in order to let us go and Carol was quite keen, Tracy who was only eighteen and had never done anything like that before, was a little reticent at first, but after talking it over, decided she would like to give it a go. So I then had the unenviable task of explaining to our youngest member that we would not be able to take her on the trip, which was hard and disappointing for her, but I felt the opportunity to do something to cheer up our forces after the war and experience a big adventure, was not to be missed. We were to be on a show that would be wholly self contained with no road manager or representative from CSE as normal and totally in the organisational hands of the Royal navy, who's code name for the show was "Operation Showboat".

Before we departed the local television 6.30 pm news programme invited the girls and I on to the show to be interviewed. After the interview they wished us luck and asked me to come back again to report on how the shows went on our return.

We would be flying out early one morning from RAF Brize Norton in Oxfordshire and would therefore need to stay somewhere in the vicinity the night before. At first I thought a hotel but then I remembered that Kenny Lynch lived in the area and his offer of accommodation, so I called him and he said he would be only too pleased to have us stay overnight at his house. When we arrived he said "I've cooked a chicken" and we were pleased to think we were getting supper as well. But he meant it literally, he had simply cooked a chicken, which he then placed on the coffee table and gave us plates and cutlery to help ourselves. Typical bachelor I guess, but it was most welcome anyway. One of Kenny's cats had apparently recently given birth to kittens underneath his bed and the next morning they appeared and we got to give them a cuddle before leaving for the airport.

Chapter 12

OPERATION SHOWBOAT

We only got to meet our fellow artistes on the show when we arrived at RAF Brize Norton prior to flying out to Ascension Island - comedian/ singer Bobby Knutt and husband and wife crazy comedy team Roger l'Idiot et Ce (Celia). It was strange having no-one officially in charge of the show, so we literally had to put our heads together and work out the format between us on the way and we were grateful to Bobby who had brought along a superb sound system and microphones which he provided for the whole show to use. The situation meant we had to get on well together and we did.

Some official photos were taken of us all boarding the plane at the start of our journey, with Carol, Tracy and I high kicking at the top of the aircraft steps, which were sent to us all later (the photographs that is, not the steps.) Being on a military plane is strange because the seats all face backwards for safety reasons and so taking off and landing feel quite weird. We had one brief stop on the way touching down at Dakar Airport in Senegal where we were able to get off the plane and walk around in the fresh air for a while.

When we arrived on Ascension Island, we found ourselves caught up in a flurry of activity as we were transferred, along with one thousand military personnel to M.V.Norland, the formerly Scandinavian route ferry that had been diverted to the South Atlantic in order to carry troops to and from the Falkland Islands during and after the war. As I mentioned, the airport on Port Stanley was at that time still out of service due to war damage and the fact that the Argentine troops had planted land mines all over the place. On this trip, M.V. Norland was to carry a thousand service men and women out to the Falklands to replace the serving troops who had spent the war out there and bring back those troops, plus some Falkland Islanders who wanted to visit their families in Britain and our show.

The schedule given to us from naval command was that we would perform shows over two nights on the Norland, so that an audience of about five hundred service people could watch the show each night on the voyage out and then, when we reached the waters closer to the Falkland Islands, we would be transferred by helicopter to HMS Invincible, HMS Bristol, HMS Birmingham, HMS Southampton and the troop ship MV Rangatira, after which we would return performing another two shows on the Norland during the voyage back to Ascension. This plan was actually changed slightly with an additional show, but more of that later.

We were all given cabins and allotted a steward called Raymond. In the evenings Raymond played the piano, sporting make up and liked to be known as "Wendy". He had played for the troops throughout the war, keeping up morale and had enjoyed this new role of serving on a troop carrier.

The journey would take a few days and we spent time getting to know our fellow passengers and, while we were still in the sunshine, getting a bit of sunbathing in on the topmost deck, away from view, (apart from the bridge). As we moved further south though, the weather became progressively colder and the bikinis and t shirts gave way to warm jumpers and jeans. The troops found various ways to keep themselves entertained during the trip, one day we spotted some of the "squaddies" who had rigged up makeshift fishing gear and were trying to catch Piranha from the stern.

Our first show was scheduled to begin at 20.30 hours on Friday 13th August. We set up the sound system and had worked out a programme. It was agreed that Bobby Knutt would go on first and introduce the show, the girls and I would perform a twenty minute spot, Bobby would then compere a bit more and introduce Roger and Celia who would perform forty minutes, then Bobby would reintroduce us again for another twenty minutes, followed by his main spot. Finally we would all come back on and take a bow followed by a small session of singalong songs with the audience, starting with "We Are Sailing". The sea was as smooth as glass.

At 8 p.m. we were all backstage - a curtained off area with no access except to the stage - getting ready for the show and the boat was beginning to move up and down a little. By 8.25 p.m the sea was as rough as could be, the motion was horrendous and as we were deep in the bowels of the ship with no facilities or fresh air, I became seasick and had to throw up into a plastic carrier bag. There was panic in those few minutes, however, I told Bobby to go on and introduce us as planned, then I drank some water and touched up my make up and made it to the stage on time. The girls and I performed our first spot to a very enthusiastic crowd, though Carol and Tracy were struggling a little to dance with the rocking motion of the ship. I was fine during the act but as soon as we came off stage I was immediately sick again and had to replace my all my make up once more prior to going back on for our second spot, which also went down well. Whilst Bobby was performing his act, I unfortunately threw up yet again and this time I was joined by Tracy. I felt exhausted and dehydrated by then, but we still had to perform the sing along at the end. As the main singer, I felt I should stay, but I sent a grateful Tracy back to her cabin and so just Carol and I went on at the end with Bobby, Roger and Celia. I will never forget gripping that microphone stand and singing "We Are Sailing" as long as I live. The show however received a standing ovation and the Captain, Bob Lough said later, that he hadn't realised just how rough it was until he stood up to applaud us at the end of the show. As we were sorting ourselves out back stage he sent another officer round to invite us all for a drink in his quarters, but I had to politely refuse, asking the officer if he would kindly help me back to my cabin instead as I no longer felt capable of standing up unaided, let alone walking. He was very concerned and helpful, but after a good night's sleep, I was fine and thankfully the sea was calm on the following night, no more sea sickness and the show once again went down a bomb with the audience.

During the voyage we made a lot of friends on board and a group from 202 Squadron RAF particularly took us under their wings, so to speak, we would get together with them and sing songs accompanied by Bobby on his guitar and, before we left they insisted on having a group photo taken with we three and Celia on deck.

The day came however when we were due to be transported on a 100 mile trip by Sea King helicopter to HMS Invincible, first though we all had to be kitted out in "goon suits". These were bright orange all-in-one waterproof suits (with feet) and hoods, plus life jackets and they were all man sized so they felt huge on us. This was just in case the helicopter had to ditch into the sea. We stood on deck awaiting their arrival and soon two Sea Kings came into view, the first one took all the equipment and our bags and the second carried us. We had to wear ear protectors inside the helicopter due to the noise, which kind of topped the whole outfit off nicely. Eventually we landed on the deck of the aircraft carrier Invincible in a high wind and after being welcomed by a senior officer, we huddled together as that section of the deck then hydraulically lowered into the hangar below where all the harrier jets were kept, and where men were busily erecting a stage for us to perform on later. We were relieved of the goon suits and shown to our cabins. After we had washed and changed prior to the show, we met up in the hangar and Captain J.J. Black made a welcome speech and presented us all with signed prints of the ship, along with Invincible hats, t-shirts and believe or not, knickers with "Invincible" written across the front. We were then introduced to some of the other officers including H.R.H. Prince Andrew who was a serving helicopter pilot on Invincible at that time. He shook hands with Carol and I and then asked us what other ships we would be performing our shows on, I politely listed the names of the various Royal Navy vessels and also the MV Rangatira and he retorted "Not the Rangatira! It smells like a bloody shithouse!" As Carol and I stared open mouthed at the prince, he went on to explain that the ship's desalination plant had broken down causing the water to smell bad. He then wished us luck with the performances and continued to circulate, having a word with us all. Then, after having some light refreshments we went backstage and prepared for the show.

The two shows on Invincible were absolutely fantastic, everything went off perfectly and our audience including H.R.H. Prince Andrew who attended our second performance, were extremely appreciative. The hangar was so full that some sailors were watching from aircraft around the walls of the hangar, being the only seats left in the house. When we all came back on for the very last finale, I said to the girls "Let's put on the t-shirts and knickers over our tights to go on for a bow. As we were announced a great cheer went up from the audience, but when we actually appeared wearing the Invincible kit the cheers grew even louder with much appreciative whistling. After the sing song we all received another standing ovation which seemed to go on for ages. Captain Black came up on stage and made another speech and we all felt on a high.

He then invited us to the officer's wardroom for a steak dinner. After we had eaten, musical instruments appeared and we ended up having another sing song which went on until around 3 o'clock in the morning. Prince Andrew circulated once more, sitting with us all in turn. He also sang along with gusto, including (somewhat incongruously) heartily singing all the words to "My Old Man's a Dustman". He asked me to sing Ralph McTell's "Streets of London" for him which he said was his favourite song and one of the other officers played along on his saxophone. While the prince was talking to Carol and I, something came up in conversation that made me say "I have a terrible sense of direction, I can get lost going from the sitting room to the bathroom" to which the prince replied "You should come to our place!" It was quite amusing that to him Buckingham Palace was just "our place".

It was such a fun evening and a few photos were taken, some with my camera and some on Bobby Knutt's and afterwards I said to the girls, "we'll keep quiet about these pictures because if the press find out about them they might hound us and try to buy them, so let's not tell anyone outside of our families". The girls agreed.

The following morning, we gathered for breakfast and then struggled back into the goon suits to be taken on to HMS Southampton which was much smaller after the vastness of the aircraft carrier. H.R.H. Prince Andrew came on deck and helped us all into the helicopter and waved us off which was really great.

On HMS Southampton we performed to yet another packed audience, sailors were once again hanging from anything that would hold them and it was another successful show, we then travelled via Lynx helicopter to the Admiral's ship HMS Bristol, where we were met by Rear Admiral D.R. Reffell who presented us with a warm service jumper each (which came in very handy on Port Stanley later), and some souvenir banknotes of Falkland Isles currency. Our stage on HMS Bristol was erected in the dining hall and crammed full with yet another enthusiastic audience. We stayed overnight on board Bristol, I was in fact given the Admiral's cabin, minus the Admiral of course, and the following day we prepared to be taken once again by Lynx helicopter to the troop ship MV Rangatira, however the weather had other ideas and by the time the Lynx arrived we had 50 knot winds buffeting the ship and despite the highly experienced pilot's best efforts to land on the one small helipad of HMS Bristol, in the end he had to admit defeat. I must admit, watching him try to land on a rocking ship was quite terrifying, he obviously didn't want to let anybody down, but it was actually a relief when he gave up. However, it left the navy with the problem of how to get us onto M.V Rangatira. It transpired that there was a tug in the area and so the tug Yorkshireman was contacted and agreed to come to our rescue. The plan was that as it came alongside (in an appalling hail and wind storm), we and our equipment were all to be individually winched over the side onto its deck. This took quite some time as the two ships would keep parting company, then swing back together again, but eventually both artistes and luggage were safely aboard. Yorkshireman then sailed us out to the troop ship Rangatira, which I'm pleased to say had managed to sort out its water problems by then and there was no longer a terrible smell.

We were settled into small cabins and the next day we had to perform three shows for all the troops aboard. The audience on this ship was made up of about 95% troops both army and air force and 5% off duty merchant seamen who were part of the Rangatira's crew. Unfortunately the merchant men were not governed by the same rules on alcohol consumption as the troops were and a small group of them in our first audience who had been drinking constantly began to make a lot of noise, spoiling it rather for the troops in the audience who were obliged, due to their officers having no authority over the merchant men, to sit and bear it. One man was particularly obnoxious, shouting out various offensive chestnuts like "Get yer kit off" etc. It was such a shame. Before the next show we were thrilled to find that our friends from 202 squadron had also been transferred to the Rangatira and when they heard about the problems in the first show they placed themselves like guards around the stage area for the next performance. However the next two shows went really well and we had no further problems. Later we heard that the main offender from the bunch of loud mouths at our first show was laid up in the ship's hospital- it seemed someone had taken it upon themselves to "sort him out" though no-one seemed to know who and therefore nobody was put on a charge.

In the meantime, behind the scenes, messages had been going back and forth from the Army commander on the Falklands to the Admiral with a pleading request to "borrow" the show for one night on Port Stanley. There had to be quite a lot of planning for this, but in the end it was agreed that the navy would fly us by Sea King helicopters (once again in the stylish goon suits) onto RAF Stanley where the army would then take care of us overnight. The army arranged for us all to stay with an ex major and his wife who had settled in Port Stanley after his retirement from the army - 'Nidge' and Ron Buckett, who made us really welcome in their home. The show was to take place in a large marquee style tent on the airfield. Before getting ready for the show we were escorted on foot to the building which had served as Departures and Arrivals before the war as it contained toilet facilities. The building was full of Gurkhas at the time and we had to make our way through them in order to get to the loos. When we re-emerged from the building, we then had to walk back across the airfield to the marquee in which we would be performing. There was snow on the ground and the crosswinds on the airfield made walking alone nigh impossible, so we all had to link arms very tightly and walk in a solid line in order to just stay upright.

Inside the marquee a stage had been erected with a little curtained off area on each side equipped with chairs, a hanging rail and shelves, oh yes – and an empty fire bucket in case we needed the loo. It was extremely cold, but giant blow heaters had been placed outside facing the tent to try to keep the chill off. Once again the show was a great success and thankfully no-one needed the bucket, though, as we girls were fairly scantily clad, it was strange to see our audience muffled up in thick jumpers, parkas and hats.

After this much appreciated show we were driven by jeep (very carefully along a strictly marked out route as there were still land mines about) into Port Stanley where we stayed the night at Nidge and Ron's house. I think Bobby and Roger shared the only spare bedroom and we girls including Celia made a round bed on the floor in the lounge in sleeping bags, along with their very nervous cat who slept in the hearth, a spot he had apparently favoured and stayed in most of the time since becoming traumatised by the noises of war.

After a hearty breakfast, we thanked Nidge and Ron profusely for their warm hospitality before being collected and given a short tour of Port Stanley. Time for a few pics, then it was back into the goon suits once more and another Sea King helicopter ride back to MV. Norland, where Captain Bob Lough and his crew gave us a very warm welcome back.

It was a comfortable and enjoyable journey back to Ascension as the sea was much kinder on the return journey and by then we knew most of the crew. We performed two more concerts on this trip to entertain the returning soldiers along with some Falkland islanders. In turn we were also entertained with social gatherings: a dinner with the Captain and, on reaching warmer waters, a barbecue on deck. Raymond (Wendy) Gibson our steward played the piano, affectionately known as Harvey, and which was later brought to the Parachute Regiment's Museum as a war relic as the keys were seizing up. Many troops who had travelled on MV Norland during and after the war said they would have been pretty miserable without the nightly sing songs when Ray had played the piano for them, even when they were under fire. However there had been a whip round and we were pleased to be at the official presentation of the money presented to Raymond for a new piano.

We also spent time talking to some of the Islanders who were travelling back to Blighty, they all had interesting stories to tell about the Invasion. One farmer's wife told us that she had comforted one Argentinian "soldier" who was about 15 years old and in tears as he and his young colleagues had been taken out of school and thought they were coming to "rescue" the Islanders from the British, but were astonished to find contented British people who spoke only English, not Spanish, and did not want to be rescued.

There were many emotional farewells following that tour which, without doubt was one of the most amazing experiences in all our lives.

On October 28th 1982 a letter was printed in The Stage newspaper from the F & CPO's Mess, HMS Bristol which read:

SIR, I don't know if you were aware of the artistes that went "South" to entertain the servicemen during the Falkland's Conflict. If so I apologise for repetition. The show was put on for us under extremely severe weather conditions. That and the makeshift stages and other temporary facilities did not stop the group putting on a terrific non-stop three hour show. I can vouch for the ship's company of HMS Bristol and say that they really cheered us up. They were a credit to your profession. Now they will have gone their separate ways, but for hundreds of servicemen they will not be forgotten. I wanted to say thank you to someone for six true entertainers.   John Earle.

We had many messages of thanks, but that one particularly touched me.

On our return home the local T.V. wanted to do a follow up interview with me which was arranged for a few days later. Our photographs were developed and though newspapers kept ringing up asking whether we had shots of Prince Andrew, as agreed we always emphatically said "no". Then one day, Bobby Knutt who was chatting to Carol on the phone, said "Oh by the way, I'm afraid I let it slip that we took photos". Then all hell broke loose. The press began bombarding Combined Services Entertainments office and, as I refused to answer the phone, were also constantly bothering Stephen in the office, one reporter even turned up on our doorstep and took one of our publicity photos from the office wall. Then Stephen received a call from The Sun informing him that the Mirror was in the process of buying Bobby Knutt's photos so we may as well sell mine to the Sun as they would be in print anyway. All this was by then driving him insane and he couldn't get any work done, every time he answered the office phone it was the tabloids and so Stephen asked me if there was anything embarrassing in the photos, I replied "Of course not, they were just taken during a sing song session in the Officer's Mess".

So in the end I reluctantly gave in and let the Sun have one negative strip which had four photos on it, one with Prince Andrew sitting with an arm around Carol and one arm around me, although this only happened for a moment when the prince had said, "let's pose properly".

I went to the studios and did my interview with Southern T.V. and while I was in make up, the Sun newspaper called me and did a very brief interview over the telephone. The live interview on T.V. was great because people heard me saying precisely what I had actually said, no-one else twisted my words. Not so with the newspapers.

I could not believe the spread in the Sun, and the way they had changed everything I had said to something completely different. By the way they used all the photos, much enlarged, they had managed to present a totally different view of the truth. After what we had been through on that tour and all it had meant to us as performers and to the troops we entertained, the Sun had reduced it to glamorous inane tripe and I was devastated. We were on the whole of the front page and the centre page spread. Then other papers picked up the story and equally daft things were written and to top it all, Bobby Knutt said afterwards that he had never agreed to sell his pictures to the Mirror or anyone else, although I did hold him responsible for letting the cat out of the bag in the first place.

I even wrote to Buckingham Palace, apologising for the content of articles and assuring them that the so-called quotes from me were not my words at all. I had a nice letter back on the lines of "Don't worry, we know how the press behave and are used to it". I talked to David (Hamilton) about it and he spent a good ten minutes telling me not to let it bother me and that's the way the press are, and to take no notice. The following day, the William Hickey column of the Daily Express printed a piece saying that David Hamilton was so upset that Prince Andrew had "cuddled" his girlfriend that he had gone into a huff and was not going to invite me to his forthcoming birthday party. David then rang me really annoyed with the Express and ranting about this article and what rubbish it was and so on, I could only say "hang on, you spent ages yesterday telling me to take no notice of them". The truth was that when they had phoned David to ask him what he thought of Prince Andrew putting his arm round his girlfriend, David had simply said "Shows the man has good taste". But they made up their own drivel and I guess it doesn't matter how famous or not you are, the gutter press can still twist everything and get to you.

I did of course attend David's party, which was held in Maidstone and it was amazing how many people suddenly wanted to take pictures of us together. People I barely knew were suddenly my best friends. This didn't sit well with me at all. I felt I had opened Pandora's Box and when this burst of fame jumped out, it bit me.

Fortunately, when Prince Andrew arrived back home and the press discovered his girlfriend's identity – American actress Koo Stark, all their attention was suddenly diverted. They managed to spoil their romance by digging up the soft porn movie she had once made. Needless to say I have never picked up or read The Sun newspaper from that day to this and I never read celebrity gossip because I simply would not believe most of it.

Chapter 13

A NEW RECORD, THE FINAL SUMMER SEASON & A WEDDING

Life goes on of course. Stephen, along with Linda's husband Graeme at the recording studio thought it would be a good idea for me to make a solo record. So we found a song and I went to the studios and started to rehearse it. Somehow over the session the sound and style of the song began to change until I was putting on a little girlie voice and the overall effect was quite punkish. Then when everyone thought it was great, they decided I should record it under a false name with a new image to match the rather crazy lyrics. So I morphed into a creation called Angel Eek and had punk/glam make up, a silver lame gymslip and tie with white ankle socks and had photos taken, the record was pressed and was hawked around to the radio stations by a professional pusher. David thought it was good and I did mime to it in a guest spot on one of his live gigs, but despite that, the Radio 2 panel wouldn't put it on their play list as they said it was too Radio 1, and Radio 1 wouldn't take it for their play list as they said it was too Radio 2. There were no opportunities on line in those days, so without the play list acceptance many good records went unheard by the public. I sent a copy of it to some friends in America who had four children between the ages of 9 and 16 and they apparently played it incessantly for weeks. They loved it.

It was frustrating at the time, but looking back, it was just a novelty, NOT the real me and even if it had got the air play, would most probably have only been a "one hit wonder".

Dream and I never returned to the Tudor House as we were shocked to find that in our absence, it had burnt down. The building was totally gutted, so that was that. We did however go out to Germany for the British forces and were made official pin ups for RAF 12 Squadron out there, following our trip to The Falklands.

Back down to earth, at Christmas we became the Flame Show again and appeared successfully for a short winter season in Blackpool.

In January, Linda and her husband Graeme invited me to a party being given by Graeme's best friend Charles at his parent's home in Chilham. I talked to Charles for quite a while and he invited me to a dinner party for his birthday with a few friends, which I accepted. That evening it snowed heavily and the roads turned treacherous, so I was persuaded not to drive home and as Charles and I did the washing up together we realised we rather liked one another. A few days later he invited me to accompany him to a friend's 21st party in London and I suppose it was what's known as a whirlwind romance. Suddenly I just knew he was the man I would marry and so I told David who was sweet about it and coincidentally within a few weeks he also met a lady who he has been with ever since. Funny how things turn out. Charles and I became engaged on 9th April 1983, but soon after I would be off to the Isle of Wight for a long summer season as Solid Gold Promotions had taken over the Ryde Pavillion for the whole summer. We would be putting on an evening show with a wild west theme, which we did not appear in, presenting lunchtime children's shows which I usually compered, and arranging entertainment in the garden area during high season, as well as being responsible for organising the catering. On top of that we were starring in our own show at the Ventnor Winter Gardens for four nights during the main season and performing two more evenings in cabaret, one at a holiday camp and one in a nightclub.

Also later in the season we had a plea for help from the Sandown Pavilion which was presenting the Jimmy Cricket show. A female singer called Elaine St. Clair who was part of their show had gone down with a bad throat infection and I was asked if I would stand in for her for a couple of nights. Apart from a 15 minute solo singing spot, I also had to learn their opening and closing numbers as Elaine performed these with the shows dancers. It all worked out well though and recently, when I was looking through old photos and papers to help with this book, I found I still have the thank you letter Elaine sent me tucked into the show programme.

So during that summer of seven day/six nights work each week, and having a fiancé visit me two or three times during the summer only to find I barely had any time to see him, I began to feel that I had had my fill of show business and what I really wanted was to settle down with a husband, home and hopefully a family. Consequently, our wedding originally planned for the following summer was brought forward to October of that year.

When we wed on October 8th, I decided to leave the business, at least for a while and concentrate on making a home. I didn't work in show business for the next few months and during that time we bought a little cottage in the Kent countryside, acquired a beautiful little kitten and got to know each other better. But there would be more singing to come.

Chapter 14

POPPY

One day Stephen rang me and asked if I would be interested in doing some promotion work, helping on the Isle of Wight's stand at the Caravan and Camping Exhibition at Birmingham NEC with Penny. I agreed, and that week Penny and I really got to know each other better than we ever had, with no rehearsals to take up our time. At that time Penny was working with another girl in a double act called Poppy, but she and her partner were having problems and not getting on at all, so she said they would be splitting up, leaving Penny to cancel the gigs they had lined up.

I said that would be a shame and tentatively suggested I join her for these few last gigs and Penny agreed. So we rehearsed Poppy's songs at my house, much to the fascination of our cat, who would sit in front of us staring then suddenly roll over on her back. We would frequently collapse into laughter at her antics.

I altered some costumes from our wardrobe store for us and we successfully completed the gigs which we enjoyed very much, however they went so well that we were offered more gigs. We decided then to carry on, extending our repertoire and buying some new outfits. Towards the end of 1985, we were asked if we would fly out to India to perform on new year's eve at the newly built Meridian Hotel in New Delhi. The hotel wasn't in fact completed as the hotel bedrooms were not finished, but they had managed to get some of the public rooms and restaurants ready for the Christmas and new year season and realised that they could now have a super function on New Year's Eve for which they would need a cabaret.

As this was quite a late arrangement, the hotel had some difficulty booking flights for us during that busy period, but eventually found us seats with Aeroflot flying via Moscow. We arrived at the airport and checked in on time, but the flight was late being called and on inquiring, we were told that the wheel had come off the plane, by a woman who gave us the distinct impression that this was not unusual for Aeroflot. When we were eventually allowed to board, the mostly Indian passengers, none of whom had been allocated seat numbers, charged forward like they do on railway stations in India, so Penny and I found ourselves swept along in a raucous free for all to get on the plane and be seated. When we took off there were still open flaps on some of the overhead baggage lockers which had not been checked by the crew. By this time, we were rapidly losing confidence in Aeroflot. However, once airborne, the first flight went smoothly and we were served a decent chicken meal on the journey. When we landed in Moscow, the airport was covered in snow and the planes had to have machines blowing hot air on to their engines to prevent them icing up before they could take off again. On the second flight we were also served a chicken meal but this one was made in Russia and was poor quality and served with stale rolls.

However, on arrival in New Delhi, in complete contrast to the journey, we were met by a representative from the Meridian Hotel and from that moment we were treated like stars. As the guest bedrooms at the Meridian were not yet completed, Penny and I were given a room on the top floor at another hotel opposite the Meridian from which we had a wonderful view of the city. In the morning, we looked out on eagles flying in the morning mist. Beautiful. We were there for three full days, but only had to work one night, New Year's eve, so the hotel management arranged for us to be shown around the city each day accompanied by a member of their staff, taking in the sights including the Red Fort, Gandhi's tomb and the wondrous streets of New Delhi with their brilliant colours, crazy traffic, snake charmers and elephants.

On New Year's eve we performed two sets in the very beautiful Napoleon suite, which was packed, the shows went down well and afterwards, we were caught up in the celebrations with all the staff backstage wishing us and each other a Happy New Year, the atmosphere was great. We enjoyed this short visit immensely, but all too soon the time came to brave the journey home again. Once more there was a complete free for all of jostling people trying to be first on the plane, pushing and elbowing their way on board. On the flight to Moscow we were again served a chicken meal, this time spicy and quite nice. However, it was night time when we landed in a freezing Moscow airport and we were informed that due to bad weather conditions we could not board the flight back to London until the morning. So we decided to have a look around the airport, that didn't take long as unfortunately there was only an odd light bulb lit up amid hundreds, creating a sort of twilight atmosphere, we did eventually find a bar that was open, but the barmaid insisted on serving all the male customers, ignoring Penny and I, until all the men had been served. After our drink we found somewhere to put our heads down until morning, when airline staff invited us into the restaurant for a complimentary breakfast. Feeling cheered by this news we joined our fellow passengers in anticipation. The breakfast turned out to consist of hard boiled eggs and salami type sausage which contained more fat than meat and a slice of hard black bread each, served with rancid butter. There was also a hot drink which could have been tea or coffee, we really couldn't tell. It was a relief to be told we could board the plane back to London.

After the usual fracas to board the plane, just to round things off nicely, we were served yet another dreadful chicken meal on that flight too.

Our time in New Delhi was wonderful, but the air travel definitely wasn't the best experience. That was however in the early '80's, I sincerely hope Aeroflot has improved since then.

Another interesting trip for Penny and I was a tour in Germany to entertain British troops stationed out there. We went over there in Penny's mini and joined up with a group called the Hillsiders, a comedian and a road manager for the tour. We got on really well with our fellow artistes, which always helps and enjoyed most of the trip. We were very impressed with the beautiful medieval town called Celle, which fortunately had not been affected by bombing during the war and so was a really attractive place to spend the day.

At that time the Berlin wall was still in place and in order for us to reach West Berlin we had to drive through part of East Germany in order to get there This meant that our vehicles had to be issued with a union jack flag, which we were to put in the window of the car in the case of a breakdown/puncture etc., and wait for roadside assistance as it was strictly "verboten" to get out of the vehicles on the eastern side. Fortunately, there were no hitches and we thankfully arrived in Berlin without incident. Whilst there, we saw the sights, shopped in Spandau and at a great flea market that was set up in the carriages of an old train and also visited the Museum at checkpoint Charlie, which was full of information about the wall and various escapes of people from the East. Interesting to hear that many escapees, having risked life and limb to reach the West, had returned to the East after struggling to survive on a low income in the affluent West. Very sad.

Whilst in Germany, we also made a very moving visit to the site of Bergen Belsen concentration camp, now raised to the ground and turned into a memorial garden, if that is the right word, as nothing would grow there except heather, and there was a noticeable lack of birdsong. The day we were there, a young German man stood waving a flag beneath a banner that said "Never Again".

During my time with Trilogy and Stephen Gold with Flame, I had appeared in twelve tours of Northern Ireland for British troops through Combined Services Entertainment, but now as Poppy, Penny and I were asked to go again. It would my thirteenth tour there. This time I was married and had someone waiting at home for me and that possibly made me more aware of the dangers, for the first time.

Following our first show there, we left the army base and went back to the hotel. The next morning we went to another base, where we were told that the first base we appeared at the previous day was mortar bombed just after we left. Later we had to be transported up the Falls Road, so were not taken by coach as per usual, but travelled inside army vehicles known as "pigs" which are a sort of cross between a small tank and a jeep. There was an opening in the roof, as in a tank, where a lookout could stand up and we were told to sit well back from this as people would try to throw all sorts of stuff into the pigs through this opening. As we drove along the Falls Road that day most of the aggressors were simply kids giving 'V' signs, but it still made for an uncomfortable journey. After that, I decided that would have to be my last CSE tour in Northern Ireland.

Chapter 15
EXTRA TIME

Penny and I did a few more gigs in England, but during this time I unfortunately suffered two miscarriages. I really hoped and believed I would have children, so decided to stop singing and dancing for a living and as I still had my Equity card, and was already signed up with a couple of agencies who booked extras, walk-ons and models, I concentrated more on this type of work which would be gentler, but still allow me to keep a foot in the business, while spending more time at home. I worked as an extra on a lot of T.V. shows and adverts, appearing several times on The Darling Buds of May as a villager, a few times on London's Burning and was a regular policewoman extra on The Bill.

I soon became pregnant again and this time at the age of 41, I gave birth to a beautiful healthy girl, Annabelle. When Annabelle was 15 months old I did a stand in job for a month on a T.V. film called The Heat of the Day starring Patricia Hodge, Sir Michael Gambon and Michael York for Granada Television. I stood in for Patricia Hodge as we have the same colour hair, so that all the camera angles and lighting could be worked out before her actual takes. She was in almost every scene and as she was pregnant at the time, my stand in role allowed her some respite. I was originally booked on the film for just a week while they were shooting in the South East, but then went on to do the final three weeks of filming in Manchester as I was able to stay with my parents. I was just there Monday to Friday, coming back home to Kent at the weekends. On one of these weekends I must have conceived my son Alex, but a spooky thing happened. When I was back in Manchester and standing on a railway station platform wearing an identical suit to Patricia, the head camera technician was holding up and reading a light meter in front of me and then he pretended he was one of these machines that tell your weight and fortune that used to be on old railway stations and joked, "You are 5'4", weigh 110 lbs, oh and you are pregnant!" and we both laughed. But it turned out to be true and almost two years to the day that I had given birth to Annabelle, my son Alex entered the world - three weeks early, but healthy.

I carried on doing walk-on work up until Alex went to school and the children often accompanied me, appearing in various T.V. ads and dramas in the background. My daughter Annabelle even "starred" in a Pampers commercial and magazine ad. At this time I also joined our local village players and appeared in amateur shows and pantomimes with them which I found I thoroughly enjoyed, and also formed a parents "rock band" appearing at all the fetes, barbecues etc. held by the primary school my children attended.

Wherever we have lived - in Kent, Wales, Shropshire and Dorset, I have joined amateur groups and/or choirs and so kept entertaining, though it is just for fun these days.

During my professional career I never found fame, apart from the short burst in the autumn of '82, but I feel I had a truly interesting and mostly enjoyable life in show business, lots of ups and downs of course, and I am proud to say in all those years, only once did I have to miss a show due to illness. I consider myself fortunate, in not only having travelled extensively, enjoyed singing and entertaining people and meeting lots of wonderful friends along the way, but also in becoming a mum to two wonderful and now grown up children.

ACKNOWLEDGEMENTS

Firstly I would like to express my gratitude to my beloved late parents for all their support in the early years of my career, for allowing so many singers, group members and musicians into their home for rehearsals and practise, always with a warm welcome and for keeping every single postcard and airmail letter I ever sent them from different parts of the world, the bulk of which have now proved invaluable to me in recalling times, dates, events and many details I simply would not have remembered precisely.

Thanks to my partner Ian for reading early drafts and making suggestions and for helping me with the scanning of photos and all his encouragement.

Finally my grateful thanks to Chella Adgopul at Honeybee Books for all her help and expertise in publishing the final book.